Contents

D1157787

Contents
Higher Scores on Reading and Language Arts, Grade 4

Introduction

This book is a tool to give your students practice in taking standardized tests. Research shows that students who are acquainted with the scoring format of standardized tests score higher on those tests. The concepts presented in this book are typically found on standardized tests in Reading and Language Arts for this grade level. The goal of this book is to improve students' ability to perform well on standardized tests. Students will have multiple opportunities to practice answering items in multiple-choice format, as well as to respond to open-ended items and writing prompts.

The tracking progress charts can help you pinpoint areas of weakness and strength with particular skills.

The book is divided into two main sections. The first section includes Test Tips and Practice for four main areas: Reading, Language Arts, Vocabulary, and Writing. Test Tips provide a review of common skills and terms as well as strategies related to the topic. The Reading section focuses on literary texts (stories, poems, and drama) and informational texts (nonfiction and technical). The Language Arts section covers grammar, usage, and mechanics, as well as editing and revising skills. The Vocabulary section covers skills related to vocabulary acquisition, such as using context clues to determine the meaning of unfamiliar words and analyzing word relationships. The Writing section focuses on three types of writing prompts: opinion, informative, and narrative.

The second section provides Practice Tests for each area. For an authentic testing experience, students will record their answers to test items on an answer sheet.

Tracking Progress Chart

Objective	Practice Item	Test Item	Mastery Yes	Mastery No	Comments
Literary Texts					
Understand and analyze plot.* (RL.4.3)	13, 17	2, 13			
Understand and analyze characters.* (RL.4.3)	3, 18	7, 14			
Understand and analyze setting.* (RL.4.3)	4	8			
Understand and analyze theme.* (RL.4.2)	9, 15	21			
Understand and analyze point of view.* (RL.4.6)	25, 29	1, 18			
Understand and analyze elements of poetry.* (RL.4.5)	20, 21, 23, 24	20			
Understand and analyze style.	8, 28				
Understand and analyze literary devices.		10, 23			
Understand and analyze elements of drama.	16	12			
Make inferences from literary texts.* (RL.4.1)	1, 7, 11, 14	6, 9, 16, 19			
Analyze and understand elements and structures of literary texts.	27	5			
Identify specific details and events in a literary text.* (RL.4.3)	2, 12, 26	3, 4, 22			
Identify and understand mythological allusions.* (RL.4.4)	5				
Identify and understand connotative and figurative use of language in literary texts.* (RL.4.4)	10, 19, 22	11, 17, 24			
Summarize literary texts.* (RL.4.2)	6	15			

*Aligned with Common Core State Standards

Objective	Practice Item	Test Item	Mastery Yes	Mastery No	Comments
Informational Texts					
Identify the main idea of a text and the details that support it.* (RI.4.2)	2, 19	6			
Analyze an author's perspective, argument, and point of view.	10, 20	3, 11			
Analyze how text structures of informational texts contribute to the development of ideas.* (RI.4.5)	6, 16	5			
Make generalizations from a text.	14				
Make inferences from an informational text.* (RI.4.1)	9, 15, 22, 26	1, 9			
Analyze and understand elements and features of informational texts.* (RI.4.3)	8, 18	14			
Summarize informational texts.* (RI.4.2)	7, 25				
Identify specific details, facts, or events in a text.* (RI.4.1)	5, 11, 17, 23	2, 12, 13			
Analyze how media and graphics contribute to a topic or issue.* (RI.4.7)	1, 4, 24	7, 10			
Identify and understand academic, domain-specific, and technical words in informational texts.* (RI.4.4)	3, 13	4, 15			
Evaluate arguments and claims and how they are supported by evidence.* (RI.4.8)	12, 21	8, 16			

Objective	Practice Item	Test Item	Mastery Yes	Mastery No	Comments
Vocabulary					
Understand common idioms, adages, and proverbs.* (L.4.5)	4	3			
Identify synonyms and antonyms.* (L.4.5)	1, 8, 9	5			
Use context clues in words, sentences, and paragraphs to decode new vocabulary.* (L.4.4)	7, 13	4, 11			
Identify and understand connotative and figurative use of language.* (L.4.5)	2	2			
Identify and use correctly multiple-meaning words.* (L.4.4)	11, 12	8, 10			
Understand academic and specialized vocabulary.* (L.4.6)	6	1			
Identify and use suffixes, prefixes, and roots to understand and create words.* (L.4.4)	5, 14	6, 12			
Interpret figures of speech, such as simple similes and metaphors.* (L.4.5)	3	9			
Understand word relationships.* (L.4.5)	10	7			
Understand how to use dictionary entries to determine pronunciation and clarify meaning.* (L.4.4)	15				

Objective	Practice Item	Test Item	Mastery Yes	Mastery No	Comments
Language Conventions					
Demonstrate control of grammar, usage, and sentence structure.* (L.4.1)	18	15, 17, 18			
Use complete sentences and recognize and correct fragments and run-ons.* (L.4.1)	19	19			
Use precise words and phrases to convey ideas.* (L.4.3)	9, 17	1, 13			
Use prepositional phrases correctly.* (L.4.1)	4, 10				
Use modals correctly.* (L.4.1)	3	5, 8			
Understand agreement.	11	4			
Recognize informal language and revise using formal language.* (L.4.3)	20	20			
Use verbs correctly, including progressive tenses.* (L.4.1)	2, 6, 14	10, 14			
Use pronouns correctly, including relative pronouns.* (L.4.1)	1, 12	3, 6			
Use adjectives correctly, including ordering adjectives according to conventional patterns.* (L.4.1)	5, 8, 15	2, 7, 11			
Use frequently confused words correctly.* (L.4.1)	7, 13, 16	9			
Avoid common usage problems.		12, 16			
Demonstrate control of standard English conventions and mechanics.* (L.4.2)	25, 33, 28	22, 37			
Use capitalization correctly. *(L.4.2)	24, 27, 31, 38	23, 26			
Use punctuation correctly.* (L.4.2)	21, 30, 36	24, 25, 27, 35			
Use commas correctly.* (L.4.2)	23, 26, 37	28, 33, 36			
Use quotation marks correctly.* (L.4.2)	29, 32, 40	31, 32			
Use correct spelling.* (L.4.2)	22, 28, 34, 35, 39	21, 29, 30, 34, 38			
Writing					
Write opinion essays.* (W.4.1)	Prompt 1	Prompt 1			
Write informative/expository essays.* (W.4.2)	Prompt 2	Prompt 2			
Write narrative essays.* (W.4.3)	Prompt 3	Prompt 3			

Tracking Progress Chart
Higher Scores on Reading and Language Arts, Grade 4

Reading Test Tips
and Practice

Standardized Tests for Reading

In the Reading Practice section, you will read some general strategies for answering multiple-choice questions and open-ended questions. Then, you will review common literary terms, comprehension skills, and reading skills related to literary and informational texts. After you review the terms and skills, you will read literary and informational selections and answer questions about them.

Strategies for Answering Multiple-Choice Questions

Here are some suggestions for taking a reading test:

- **Read the selection as though you were not even taking a test.** Get a general understanding of the topic and purpose of a selection. You may not understand everything at first, but keep reading.

- **Look at the big picture.** As you read, look for the main features of the selection. Ask yourself the following questions as you read:

  - What is the title?

  - For a literary selection, such as a story, play, or poem, what is the theme or main message? For a nonfiction selection, what is the main idea?

  - What is the author's purpose for writing the selection? Is the purpose to inform, entertain, persuade, or show how to do something?

- **Next, read the questions.** This will help you know what information to look for when you reread.

- **Reread the selection.** Underline information that relates to the questions. Jot down your notes or questions in the margin as you read. You can use them to help you answer the questions.

- **Go back to the questions.** Try to answer each one in your mind before looking at the answer choices. Circle any important words in the question. This can help you understand what the question is asking.

- **Finally, read all the answer choices.** Cross out any answer choices that you know are incorrect. Then, choose the best answer. You may need to go back to the selection and look for information. Pay attention to what the question asks. For example, if it asks for a main idea, look for a choice that is a broad concept, not a narrow detail.

Strategies for Answering Open-Ended Questions

Some standard reading tests include open-ended questions. These questions do not have answers for you to choose from. Instead, you must write a response to the question. Open-ended questions can require a short answer or an extended response of multiple paragraphs. Most open-ended questions test your ability to use what you have learned from reading a selection. Here are some suggestions for answering open-ended questions:

- Read the entire selection. Pay attention to important information, such as major events and characters or main ideas and details. Jot down information you believe is important about the selection.

- Read each question carefully.

- There are some words that appear frequently in open-ended questions, such as *compare*, *contrast*, *explain*, *interpret*, *describe*, and *summarize*. Think about what the question is asking before you answer it.

- Return to the selection and skim it. Look for the details or examples that will support your answer.

- When writing your answer, be precise but brief. Refer to details from the selection. Be sure to proofread for spelling, grammar, and punctuation errors.

- If you cannot answer the question at first, skip it and return to it later.

How Open-Ended Reading Questions Are Scored

Open-ended questions are scored based on how well they meet certain criteria. Here is an example of how open-ended questions might be scored:

Score of 3: This response has a correct answer. It is supported by information from the selection. It also has specific, appropriate, and accurate details or examples.

Score of 2: This response has only a partial answer. It shows awareness of what is to be answered, and has at least one detail from the selection. Although this response attempts to provide sufficient examples, it may contain minor inaccuracies.

Score of 1: This response is incomplete. Either the question was misunderstood, or no details from the selection were included in the response. The examples are insufficient or inappropriate, and there may be major inaccuracies.

Score of 0: This response has too little information to be scored or is inaccurate in many ways. The following conditions will cause a response to receive a score of 0:

- The response is blank or too short to be scored.

- The response is off-topic.

- The response is written in a language other than English.

- The handwriting in the response is unreadable.

Test Tips for Reading Literature

Reading tests contain different types of literary selections. Literary selections can include fiction, plays, and poems. Knowing the features of different literary selections can help you understand them and answer questions about them. Here are descriptions of different types of literature:

Fiction

Fiction tells a story about made-up rather than real events. There are many types of fiction. For example, a **myth** is a type of story that usually describes a hero or famous event. Myths often explain how something came about. A **fable** is a story that teaches a lesson. Fables usually have animal characters. A **folktale** is a traditional story or legend that has been passed down orally for many generations. A **fictional diary** or **journal** tells the events in a made-up person's life. **Historical fiction** tells about a real person or event in history. Although the characters and some events might have been real, historical fiction is meant to tell a story and not simply give information about the past.

Drama

A drama is a **play**. It is a piece of literary writing meant to be performed by actors. Most plays begin with a **cast of characters**. This is a list of the different parts in the play. When you read a play, you'll see that the name of the character comes before the words the character says. Many plays also have **stage directions**. They explain what the characters are doing, where they are, and how they are saying their lines. Usually, the stage directions are in italic type, inside parentheses, to show that they are not meant to be spoken aloud.

Poetry

A poem expresses feelings and ideas or tells stories using rhythm and imagery. The author of a poem is called a **poet**. The narrator of a poem is called a **speaker**. Poetry is written in **lines**, which are the words in one row of the poem. A line of poetry is not always a complete sentence. A **stanza** in poetry is a group of lines, similar to a paragraph. A **rhyming poem** includes words that rhyme. The rhyme usually follows a pattern; for example, the same lines in each stanza will end with rhyming words. **Free verse poetry** does not have rhyming words. Lines in free verse poems may vary in length and not follow a pattern of beats.

Summarizing

Follow these steps to choose the best answer to a summary question:

Step 1: Look for the main characters, conflict, and the most important details, such as actions and events, as you read the selection slowly and carefully.

Step 2: Consider every answer choice. Get rid of those that restate a single detail from the selection, make a general statement about the selection but include no important details, or have little or nothing to do with the selection.

Step 3: Be sure that the answer you choose covers the *entire* selection. It should include the main conflict, characters, and major supporting details.

Making Inferences

You make an inference when you use what you've read in a selection and what you already know to determine something the author hasn't stated directly. Use the following steps to answer inference questions:

Step 1: Read the selection carefully.

Step 2: Locate key words and phrases in the answer choices that match similar words and phrases in the reading selection. You may be able to get rid of some answers right away.

Step 3: Confirm your answer by considering your prior knowledge about the subject of the selection.

Drawing Conclusions

You may be asked questions that begin like this: "Why do you think . . ." or "Based on the information in the selection . . ." Questions like these require you to draw a conclusion. Use the steps below to respond to these types of questions:

Step 1: Read the question to identify the topic.

Step 2: Study the answer choices, ruling out those choices that are clearly wrong.

Step 3: Reread the selection and look for evidence that supports one of the remaining answer choices.

Analyzing Character

A character is a person or animal in a story, play, or other literary work. A writer can develop a character in several different ways:

- by describing how the character looks and dresses
- by telling the reader what the character says
- by showing the reader how the character acts
- by letting the reader know the character's thoughts and feelings
- by revealing what other characters think or say about the character
- by telling the reader directly what the character is like (kind, cruel, or brave, and so on)

Identifying Setting

Setting is the time and place of a story, play, or poem. The setting can help create a mood, help you understand the story's problem, or affect the events of the plot.

Analyzing Plot

Plot is the series of events that makes up a story. Many plots have the following structure:

- An **introduction** tells who the characters are and what their **conflict**, or problem, is.
- **Complications** arise as the characters take steps to resolve the conflict.
- The plot reaches the **climax** at the most exciting moment in the story.
- The final part of the story is the **resolution**. This is when the characters' problems are solved and the story ends.

When analyzing a story or play, you can look for the story's **problem** and **solution**. Look for what happens in the selection. How do characters try to fix the problem?

Identifying Point of View

Point of view refers to who is telling a story. Two common points of view are **first person** and **third person**.

- In first-person point of view, one of the characters, using the pronoun *I*, tells the story. The reader can know only what the narrator knows or observes.
- In third-person point of view, the narrator knows everything about the characters and events in a story.

Analyzing Theme

The theme of a story is the main message, lesson, or truth about life that the author is trying to express. A theme is not usually stated directly in the work. You will have to make an inference about a work's theme based on characters and events. Follow these steps:

Step 1: Think about the main problem in the story and how the characters react to it.

Step 2: Ask yourself if the characters learned any lesson about life or made any discoveries about themselves, others, or the world around them.

Step 3: Choose the answer that describes the overall message of the selection.

Analyzing Tone

An author's tone is how he or she sees the world or events in a literary work. Authors create a tone through their choice of words and examples. For example, the author might include examples of scary situations to create a tone of suspense. Use the following steps to answer questions about a writer's tone:

Step 1: Look at the writer's choice of words and examples. What do they tell you about the writer's attitude toward the subject?

Step 2: Read all the answer choices. Get rid of answer choices that are not supported by the author's word choices and examples.

Step 3: Reread the remaining answer choices. Choose the one that best describes the tone of the selection.

Identifying Literary Devices

Literary devices are techniques writers use to help you imagine the topic. Here are some common literary devices you might see in reading test selections:

Alliteration—repetition of the same or very similar consonant sounds in words that are close together.

> **Example:** Something moved in the deep, dark dungeon.

Allusions—references to famous works, for example, places or characters from Greek and Roman mythology.

> **Example:** Dan clicked on a link on the website, and, like a Trojan horse, the computer virus took over his computer.

Connotative language—language that creates a certain image or feeling in a reader's mind. Notice the difference in the language in the two example sentences.

> **Examples:** A family of mice settled into the barn. An army of mice invaded the barn.

Figurative language—describes one thing in terms of another.

    A **metaphor** compares one thing to something quite unlike it.

    Example: The clouds were puffs of cotton floating across the sky.

    A **simile** compares two unlike things using *like* or *as*.

    Example: Emily stood like an oak tree when the wave crashed against her.

    Personification gives human qualities to an object, plant, or animal.

    Example: The leaves whispered softly in the breeze.

Imagery—language that creates a picture in the mind using any of the five senses: sight, touch, smell, hearing, and taste.

    Example: The fireworks popped and crackled, and then a shower of bright, shimmering lights drifted down toward the ground.

Rhyme—repetition of accented vowel sounds and all sounds following them.

    Examples: mind/grind; know/show

Literature

In this selection, a girl takes a trip to an aquarium, a place where people can view many different plants and animals that live in water. Read the selection. Then, answer the questions. On your answer sheet, darken the circle for each correct answer for multiple-choice items. For the open-ended item, write your answer on a separate sheet of paper.

A Trip to the Aquarium

Anna usually slept until the last possible minute, but today was different. Anna's mother came to wake her and found her already dressed and ready to go.

"What's going on?" asked her mother.

"Today's the field trip!" Anna exclaimed.

Mr. Giannaro's fourth-grade class was going to visit the aquarium. Anna had been looking forward to this trip for months. She hoped to study the lives of fish and other sea creatures when she got older. She had seen TV shows that showed their underwater world. Today, though, would be her first chance to see these amazing animals for herself.

Everyone seemed excited about the special day, even Mr. Giannaro. He was wearing a tie with tiny pictures of whales. During the bus trip to the aquarium, Anna told her seatmate, Angela, that she wanted to see the dolphins.

"I don't like big fish," said Angela. "I like angelfish."

"Dolphins aren't really fish. They breathe air," Anna explained. She described the tricks that they could do, but nothing she said persuaded Angela.

When the class arrived, Janet, a guide at the aquarium, greeted them.

Janet took them to see many different tanks. First, they saw what looked like big flowers with fish swimming around them. Janet explained that the flowers were really animals. Next, they saw a tank filled with many brightly colored fish.

"Look at the angelfish!" exclaimed Angela.

After they had seen jellyfish, sea turtles, and strange-looking manta rays, Janet told the class that they had another surprise coming.

"We're going to see a seal show," Janet said. Anna frowned. She asked Janet whether they would also see the dolphins.

"You'll have to come back tomorrow to see them," said Janet. "Only the seals perform today."

The seals put on a wonderful show. They jumped out of the water to catch fish. One of the seals jumped through a hoop. Then Janet got two seals to bounce a ball back and forth. The class clapped and laughed at the seals' tricks.

As the class went downstairs for their lunch, Janet and Mr. Giannaro stopped Anna. "I hear you're interested in underwater animals," Janet said.

"Yes. This is an amazing place!" Anna replied. "I only wish I could see the dolphins, too."

"Well, we'll have to go home pretty soon. But you can see the dolphins for a minute. Janet has offered to show them to you," Mr. Giannaro told her.

Janet took Anna down some stairs and unlocked a door. Anna saw a tall man next to a big pool with his arms upraised. For a moment, Anna imagined the man was Poseidon ruling over the undersea world. She watched as a dolphin made a spectacular leap out of the water and through the hoop the man was holding. When the man turned, Janet introduced Anna to the head dolphin trainer, Steve. Steve showed Anna the five dolphins and explained how they used sound to communicate underwater. Then, he gave her a small dolphin pin as a gift.

When she joined the rest of her class, Anna showed her pin proudly to Angela, who had a postcard with an angelfish on it. "This is the best field trip ever," Anna thought happily.

1. Why does Anna frown when she hears about the seal show?

   A She wants to go home.

   B She is afraid of seals.

   C She wants to see the dolphins.

   D She left her lunch on the bus.

2. Why was Anna looking forward to the field trip?

   A She was going to see sea creatures in person.

   B She was going to spend the day with Angela.

   C She was going to see a movie about the underwater world.

   D She was going to meet a dolphin trainer.

3. How did Anna feel before the trip?

   A angry

   B tired

   C excited

   D nervous

4. Where does this selection mostly take place?

   A in Anna's house

   B at an elementary school

   C on a school bus

   D at an aquarium

5. Why does Anna think of Poseidon when she sees the dolphin trainer?

   A The man looks old.

   B The man seems powerful.

   C The man is swimming in the pool.

   D The man has a loud voice.

6. Which of the following is the **best** summary of the selection?

   A Anna gets up early because she is excited about the field trip. She has seen sea creatures on TV shows and wants to study them when she gets older.

   B Anna goes on a school field trip to an aquarium. She sees underwater creatures and watches a seal show. Then, Anna gets to see the dolphins.

   C At the aquarium, Anna sees animals that look like flowers. Then, she sees angelfish, jellyfish, sea turtles, and manta rays.

   D Anna gets to see the dolphins at the aquarium. She meets the head dolphin trainer, learns how dolphins communicate, and gets a small dolphin pin as a gift.

7. What made Anna's day at the aquarium so special? Give two reasons.

In this selection, a frontier family travels across the mountains to start a new life in the wilderness of Kentucky. Read the selection. Then, answer the questions. On your answer sheet, darken the circle for each correct answer for multiple-choice items. For the open-ended item, write your answer on a separate sheet of paper.

Walking the Wilderness Road

Jesse smelled the strong scent and hoped there was time to warn his younger brother. He turned and ran, almost knocking Bobby over. Both of them yelled as the skunk appeared. The boys sprinted down the hill, the wind whipping at their faces. They were only feet in front of the foul odor at their heels.

"Jess, this isn't fun anymore!" Bobby wailed.

By the time the boys reached the tent, tears flowed down Bobby's cheeks.

"What is going on here?" their mother asked.

"We were playing in the woods, and Bobby scared a skunk," Jesse replied.

Helen Dantzler softly rubbed her youngest son's head. "The skunks will stay far away from us on our journey. We'll be traveling in a big group with scores of other folks. Now, finish packing your bundles."

Two weeks later, the Dantzlers marched through the Appalachian Mountains on the Wilderness Road alongside four other families. Their possessions were strapped onto packhorses. Jesse and Bobby struggled to keep the animals on the rocky path.

It was 1784, and the Dantzlers sought new lands on the Kentucky frontier. The road they traveled had been cleared only nine years before by a group led by the famous pioneer Daniel Boone. Since then, hundreds of families had followed the boulder-strewn trail through the mountains.

"Dad, did Daniel Boone have this much trouble?" Jesse asked.

"You can ask him yourself, son," Joseph Dantzler replied. "There's word that he's settled in his old fort along the Kentucky River."

Two days later, Jesse Dantzler got his answer from Daniel Boone.

"You probably had better luck than I did with packhorses, young fella!" the famous frontiersman laughed. Jesse smiled.

Another frontier family had begun life in Kentucky.

8. Why did the author include facts about how the Wilderness Road was cleared?

   A to make the reader think about wildlife

   B to persuade the reader to move to the wilderness

   C to make the story seem more realistic

   D to explain how to build a trail

9. Which statement **best** states the theme of this selection?

   A Traveling in a group is easier than traveling alone.

   B Daniel Boone was a brave American pioneer.

   C The natural world is both wonderful and dangerous.

   D Families faced difficulties to start a new life on the frontier.

10. Read this sentence from the selection.

> The boys sprinted down the hill, the wind whipping at their faces.

Why does the author describe the wind this way?

   A to show how it stirs up the leaves on the forest floor

   B to show how it lashes against the boys' skin

   C to show how it carries the bad smell from the skunk

   D to show how it gently touches the boys as they run

11. Why does Helen Dantzler rub Bobby's head?

   A She wants to ease his headache.

   B She wants to make him fall asleep.

   C She wants to remove the skunk's spray.

   D She wants to comfort him.

12. What made the journey difficult for the Dantzlers? Give three examples from the selection.

This play is about a girl named Lucy who learns how to plant tulip bulbs. Read the play. Then, answer the questions. On your answer sheet, darken the circle for each correct answer for multiple-choice items. For the open-ended item, write your answer on a separate sheet of paper.

Planting Tulips

Characters:

LUCY MONROE

NITA LOPEZ

MRS. LOPEZ (Nita's grandmother)

MRS. MONROE (Lucy's mother)

(Lucy is playing hopscotch on the sidewalk in front of her house. Nita walks out of the house next door with her grandmother.)

NITA: Hi, Lucy! My grandma is going to teach me how to plant tulips. Want to learn, too?

LUCY: No, thanks. I'm going to watch TV.

(Lucy runs stage left and inside her house. Mrs. Monroe is standing by the door. It is obvious she was listening, and she doesn't look happy.)

MRS. MONROE: Why don't you want to learn how to plant tulips?

LUCY: I'd rather watch TV.

MRS. MONROE: You watch too much TV. That's so nice of Mrs. Lopez to offer to teach you how to garden. You should go back over there.

LUCY: *(Whining)* But Mom . . .

MRS. MONROE: Go!

(Lucy runs through the door and then stage right. She goes around the fence to where Nita and Mrs. Lopez are kneeling on the ground.)

LUCY: *(Pouting)* My mom says I should learn how to garden.

MRS. LOPEZ: *(Smiling)* I would love to teach you, Lucy! Just grab that trowel and dig a small hole in the dirt. Make sure you dig down about six inches.

(Lucy frowns before grabbing a trowel and kneeling on the ground next to Nita. She digs a hole.)

MRS. LOPEZ: That looks great! Now drop the bulb in the hole and cover it up with dirt, like this.

(Mrs. Lopez demonstrates for the girls, and then Lucy and Nita happily follow her lead.)

LUCY: *(Standing and brushing dirt off her hands)* That was really fun! I can't wait to see the garden.

NITA: When will the flowers bloom?

MRS. LOPEZ: The tulips won't actually grow until next spring. We plant the bulbs in the fall because they will grow better if they are in the ground all winter.

NITA: *(Looking sad)* Oh, I thought we'd get to see them right away.

(A clap of thunder sounds. Nita, Lucy, and Mrs. Lopez are startled and look up.)

NITA: *(Alarmed)* Grandma! Our tulips!

MRS. LOPEZ: They'll be okay. The rain will help them grow, and next spring we'll have a beautiful garden!

LUCY: Thanks for showing me how to plant tulips, Mrs. Lopez. This was way more fun than watching TV.

MRS. LOPEZ: I'm glad you joined us, Lucy. But remember, our work isn't over. In the spring we're going to have to take care of the tulips so they grow to be as healthy and pretty as possible.

LUCY: *(Excited)* I can't wait!

(It starts to rain, and they run toward the house.)

13. Why does Lucy turn down Nita's invitation at first?

   A because she wants to play hopscotch

   B because she is not friends with Nita

   C because she is afraid of Mrs. Lopez

   D because she wants to watch TV

14. Why does Mrs. Monroe most likely encourage Lucy to learn how to plant tulips?

   A because she needs to run some errands

   B because she wants Lucy to experience something new

   C because she thinks Lucy should make a new friend

   D because she thinks Mrs. Lopez is nice

15. Which statement **best** describes the theme of the play?

   A Gardening should only be done by adults.

   B You will never know if you like something unless you try it.

   C It is important to do whatever makes you happy.

   D If you like something, there is no need to do anything different.

16. How can you tell that this selection is a play?

   A It has a beginning, middle, and end.

   B It has characters and a setting.

   C It has parts that are spoken by different people.

   D It gives information about how to do something.

17. Why does Nita feel sad at the end of the play?

   A She thought the flowers would bloom more quickly.

   B She was worried about the thunder and the rain.

   C She did not enjoy planting the tulip bulbs.

   D She was concerned that the bulbs would freeze in the winter.

18. How does Lucy change from the beginning to the end of the play?

This poem describes the prairie, a type of grassland in the middle part of the United States. Read the poem. Then, answer the questions. On your answer sheet, darken the circle for each correct answer for multiple-choice items. For the open-ended item, write your answer on a separate sheet of paper.

The Prairie

I live in the part of the country

Where the little house was built.

Pioneers who first viewed this land

Saw it as a sea of grass.

When the wind blows the grass,

It ripples like ocean waves

Not large enough to splash.

When the wind blows the grass,

The grass whispers back.

It's a soft lullaby

Of sun and wind and rain.

When the wind blows the grass,

I feel like a single blade

Coaxed to bend like all the rest.

19. In this poem, how is the prairie like a sea of grass?

   A The wind makes the grass ripple like waves.

   B The grass feels soft and wet like the ocean.

   C The prairie has no plants growing on it.

   D The prairie and the sea are the same color.

20. What does the poet compare herself to in the poem?

   A a house on the prairie

   B a blade of grass

   C a sunflower

   D a ship at sea

21. Which of these techniques does the poet use in this poem?

   A rhyming words

   B a regular pattern of beats

   C repetition of lines

   D use of a single stanza

22. Why does the poet describe the sound of the grass as a lullaby?

   A to show how strong the wind is

   B to show how it is like a child

   C to show how soothing it is

   D to show how hot the sun is

23. How does the poet help readers imagine what the prairie is like?

In this poem, a boy goes on a trip to the zoo. Read the poem. Then, answer the questions. On your answer sheet, darken the circle for each correct answer for multiple-choice items. For the open-ended item, write your answer on a separate sheet of paper.

My Zoo Trip

My mother made a promise,

to take me to the zoo.

As our trip got closer,

my excitement grew and grew.

First we saw the lions,

they were sitting in the shade.

The mother lion watched,

as the cubs ran and played.

Next we watched the monkeys,

swinging through the trees.

They looked like they were having fun,

and then I think I saw one sneeze.

Then we saw the snakes,

slithering through the weeds.

One hid in a hollow log,

I think it winked at me.

Our zoo trip was so much fun,

I loved all of the creatures.

I think that when I grow up,

I'll be a great zookeeper!

24. Which words in the poem are a rhyming pair?

   A promise, closer

   B snakes, log

   C swinging, slithering

   D zoo, grew

25. Which word shows that the poem is written in first-person narration?

   A they

   B I

   C mother

   D it

26. Why does the speaker want to become a zookeeper?

   A He talks to the zookeeper during his visit.

   B His father is a zookeeper.

   C He enjoys his trip to the zoo.

   D The zoo needs someone to help with the animals.

27. What is the author's purpose for writing this poem?

   A to entertain readers with an enjoyable poem

   B to describe the snakes at the zoo in poetic language

   C to get readers to give money to the zoo

   D to teach people about different animals at the zoo

28. What kind of tone does the poet use to describe the zoo in this poem?

   A playful

   B relaxing

   C tense

   D fearful

29. How does the speaker in the poem feel about his trip? Give three examples from the poem to support your response.

Test Tips for Reading Informational Texts

Identifying the Main Idea and Supporting Details

The main idea is the central thought or the most important point. Supporting details give more information about the main idea. Sometimes the main idea is stated directly at the beginning of a selection. In other cases, you must think about the information that is presented to figure out the main idea. Follow these steps to identify the main idea:

Step 1: Read the selection. Determine the topic, or what the selection is about.

Step 2: Look for the important details in the selection. Think about what the details have in common. The details should point to the main idea.

Step 3: State the main idea in your own words. Then, look for an answer that closely matches your own. Be careful not to select a detail that merely *supports* the main idea as your answer. Also remember that the main idea reflects the entire selection, not just one paragraph or one section.

Step 4: Check to make sure that the details in the selection support your answer.

Identifying Author's Purpose

Authors have different reasons, or purposes, for writing. They may write to entertain, to express ideas, to inform, to instruct, or to persuade. In most nonfiction selections, the author's purpose is to inform, instruct, or persuade. Use the steps below for help in answering questions about purpose:

Step 1: Look in the text for clues such as the ones below.

- illustrations, diagrams, maps, charts, and headings: **to inform**

- numbered or bulleted lists, steps for doing something, and how-to selections: **to instruct**

- words like *should* and *must*, letters to the editor or a person in charge, and words that express opinions such as *good*, *worst*, and *best*: **to persuade**

- frequent use of the word *I*, emotional words, feeling words: **to express**

- description that tells a story, dialogue, rhymes, drama, or humor: **to entertain**

Step 2: Look for the response that most closely matches the general purpose you have identified.

Identifying Point of View

An author can also have a particular point of view about a topic. A point of view is the way an author looks at a topic. Follow these steps to identify the point of view:

Step 1: Look for positive or negative words when the author describes a topic. Also look for statements about what the author believes.

Step 2: Answer the question about point of view in your own words.

Step 3: Look for the choice that best matches your own answer.

Analyzing Text Structure

A text's structure is the way the author has organized ideas. Here are four common text structures:

- **Cause and effect** focuses on what causes something to happen and what happens as a result. Some of the clue words and phrases that signal cause and effect are *because*, *since*, *so that*, *therefore*, and *as a result*.

- **Sequence** tells events in the order they happen. Look for words that signal time and order, such as *first*, *next*, *then*, and *finally*. You can also look for dates.

- **Comparison and contrast** focuses on how two or more things are alike or different. Some clue words that signal contrast are *although*, *but*, *different*, *unlike*, *however*, and *yet*. Some clue words that signal comparison are *also*, *as well*, *both*, *likewise*, *alike*, *same*, *similar*, and *too*.

- **Problem and solution** describes a problem and then offers one or more ideas for solving it.

Use the steps below to help analyze text structure:

Step 1: Look for clue words that signal the organization of the selection.

Step 2: Look for important ideas. See whether these ideas are connected in an obvious way.

Step 3: Look for the answer choice that best matches the organization.

Using Graphic Features

Graphic features such as headings, captions, and labels are designed to help readers find information. Graphic features such as maps, charts, tables, diagrams, and illustrations present information visually. When you come across graphic features, use these steps:

Step 1: Read the title, labels, captions, and legend.

Step 2: Interpret the graphic. Think about what it shows and what it helps you understand.

Step 3: Think about how the information in the graphic feature relates to the text. Look for the answer that tells information about the graphic.

Summarizing a Text

A summary includes the most important ideas and details from a selection. A good summary will cover the entire selection. Follow these steps to choose the best answer to a summary question:

Step 1: Look for the main idea and the most important supporting details as you read the selection slowly and carefully.

Step 2: Consider every answer choice. Get rid of those that retell only part of the selection, make a general statement about the selection but include no important details, or focus on unimportant details in the selection.

Step 3: Be sure that the answer you choose covers the *entire* selection by including the main idea and major supporting details.

Making Inferences

You make an inference when you use what you've read in a selection and what you already know to determine something the author hasn't stated directly. Use the following steps to answer inference questions:

Step 1: Read the selection carefully.

Step 2: Locate key words and phrases in the answer choices that match similar words and phrases in the reading selection. You may be able to get rid of some answers right away.

Step 3: Confirm your answer by considering your prior knowledge about the subject of the selection.

Drawing Conclusions

You may be asked questions that begin like this: "Why do you think . . ." or "Based on the information in the selection . . ." Questions like these require you to draw a conclusion. Use the steps below to respond to these types of questions:

Step 1: Read the question to identify the topic.

Step 2: Study the answer choices, ruling out those choices that are clearly wrong.

Step 3: Reread the selection and look for evidence that supports one of the remaining answer choices.

Name _____   Date _____

This selection explains how water moves in a cycle on Earth. Read the selection. Then, answer the questions. On your answer sheet, darken the circle for each correct answer for multiple-choice items. For the open-ended item, write your answer on a separate sheet of paper.

The Water Cycle

Water is always on the move. Water exists in different ways. It can be a liquid, like the water we drink. It can also be a gas. In this condition, water is called water vapor. The water cycle involves changes in the state of water. Some water is changing back and forth from one state to another all of the time.

One step in the water cycle is condensation. Condensation occurs when water vapor changes into a liquid. When it is cold enough, more water will turn from a gas to a liquid than from a liquid to a gas. The condensed water forms clouds.

As more water vapor condenses, the drops become heavier and heavier. They can become so heavy, they fall to the surface as precipitation. Precipitation is moisture falling to the surface in the form of rain, snow, hail, or sleet.

When precipitation reaches the surface of Earth, some of it soaks into the ground. Some of it also goes into oceans, lakes, or rivers. However, some of the water does not stay in the ground or in the bodies of water. That is because the sun plays a role in the water cycle.

The sun heats up the water. The heat makes the water turn into vapor. This process is called evaporation.

After water evaporates, it condenses. Then the water cycle starts all over again. That is why it is called a cycle. Like the wheels on a bicycle, a cycle is something that goes around and around continuously.

Water recycles itself by means of the water cycle. This is one reason that we do not use up Earth's supply of water. Water is always moving away from the surface and back again.

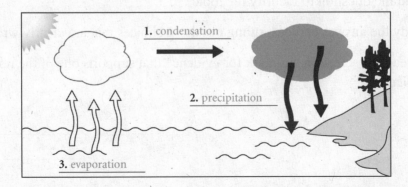

The diagram shows how water is always changing and flowing.

1. ased on information in the selection and
   he diagram, what does water do right after
   it condenses in clouds?

   A It rises from Earth as a vapor.

   B It turns into a frozen solid.

   C It evaporates into the air.

   D It falls to Earth as precipitation.

2. What is the main idea of this selection?

   A Water is always flowing and changing
      forms.

   B After water condenses, it becomes
      precipitation.

   C The sun causes the states of water to
      change.

   D In a cycle something goes around and
      around.

3. What does the word vapor mean in this
   selection?

   A idea

   B cold

   C gas

   D cycle

4. According to the diagram, where does water
   go when it first evaporates?

   A into the sun

   B into a body of water

   C into the ground

   D into the air

5. What must happen in order for water in the
   air to condense?

   A There must be clouds in the sky.

   B The temperature must be cold enough.

   C There must be rain or other
      precipitation.

   D The sun must heat the water.

6. What happens to some precipitation as it
   falls to Earth's surface?

   A It bounces back into the air.

   B It soaks into the ground.

   C It is used up and no longer available.

   D It turns into oxygen.

7. Summarize the steps in the water cycle.

Name _____ Date _____

This selection tells what home life was like long ago, before the United States became a country. Read the selection. Then, answer the questions. On your answer sheet, darken the circle for each correct answer for multiple-choice items. For the open-ended item, write your answer on a separate sheet of paper.

A Colonial Home

New England is on the eastern coast of the United States. The region is called New England because many of the first people to move there came from across the Atlantic Ocean from England.

Life was very difficult in New England during colonial times. The winters were long and cold. Wild animals roamed the woods. Many Indian tribes lived and hunted in nearby woods. People had to make, build, or grow most of the things they needed for daily life.

When the first colonists, or settlers, arrived, the men cleared spaces for their homes. They cut down trees and used them to build log cabins. The first cabins were not very warm in winter. The wind blew through the cracks, and often snow blew in. Sometimes people found their beds covered with snow. Soon the colonists learned to make their cabins warmer. They filled the cracks with chips of wood and packed them with clay. This kept out the wind and snow.

Most colonial cabins had only one room. The whole family had to cook, eat, and sleep in that single space. Most of the furniture was made by the men. Tables were often made of long boards cut from trees. Other furniture consisted of benches, spinning wheels for making yarn, and beds.

Colonial women had a lot of work to do, too. They made clothes for their families. First they had to spin the yarn, and then they had to weave the yarn into cloth. Women also made soap and the candles used for lighting the homes. They also did the cooking, which began early in the morning over a wood fire.

The fireplace was kept burning all day. At night it burned low. When people cleared out the ashes, they kept a few hot coals to start a new fire. If their fire went out, they had to borrow some hot coals from their neighbors so they could start a new fire.

People helped each other in many ways. If a family had more food than they needed, they shared it with another family. Mothers often had to leave their children at home alone while they went to nurse a neighbor who was ill.

8. Which of these would be a good title for the selection?

  A Hard Life in Colonial Times

  B Building a Log Cabin

  C Women's Work in Colonial America

  D Types of Homes in Early America

9. Why was it important to have a spinning wheel in the cabin?

  A Women could have something to do during the day.

  B Women had to spin yarn to weave into cloth.

  C Women could make fancy clothing for their families.

  D Women could make clothes for their shops.

10. Which statement describes how the author most likely feels about life in colonial America?

  A He is curious about why people moved there.

  B He is amazed by the homes people built.

  C He is confused by the jobs people did.

  D He admires how hard people worked.

11. What was the problem with the first log cabins?

  A They were built too close together.

  B Wild animals lived in the woods nearby.

  C The fire couldn't be kept burning all day.

  D Wind and snow blew through the cracks.

12. Which statement **best** supports the idea that life was challenging for colonial Americans?

  A Men made cabins for their families.

  B People had to make almost everything they needed.

  C Fires were used for heat as well as cooking.

  D Many of the first colonists came to America from England.

13. What does the word cleared mean in this selection?

  A became nicer and more pleasant

  B gave approval

  C removed trees and objects

  D passed over or through

14. What generalizations can you make from the selection about how men's and women's roles were different? Support your response with evidence from the selection.

This selection describes how to make a breakfast pizza. Read the selection. Then, answer the questions. On your answer sheet, darken the circle for each correct answer for multiple-choice items. For the open-ended item, write your answer on a separate sheet of paper.

Breakfast Pizza

Making a breakfast pizza is easy and fun. Just follow these steps, and you will have a delicious breakfast in no time!

Ingredients:

- 8-ounce can crescent rolls

- 10 ounces shredded cheddar cheese

- 3 eggs

- ¾ cup milk

- ½ to 1 pound of bacon

First, have an adult heat the oven to 425 degrees and help you cook the bacon in a pan until it is crisp. Put the bacon on a plate and let it cool. Grease a 13 x 9 inch pan with butter. Lay the rolls out flat at the bottom of the pan to make the crust. Then, scatter cheese over the crust. In a bowl, mix together the milk and eggs. Pour the milk and egg mixture over the cheese. Break up the crisp, cooled bacon and scatter it on top. Ask an adult to put the dish in the oven for you. Bake the pizza for 15 to 18 minutes. Serve immediately!

Makes six servings.

15. Why should you serve the pizza immediately?

    A so the eggs don't go bad

    B so the bacon doesn't get too crispy

    C so it doesn't get moldy

    D so it's still hot

16. What is the main way information in this selection is organized?

    A by telling the effects of having a good breakfast

    B by giving the steps you should follow in order

    C by telling a problem and describing a solution

    D by comparing different ways to make pizza

17. How many servings of breakfast pizza does the recipe make?

    A one

    B four

    C six

    D nine

18. What is the purpose of the list at the beginning of the selection?

    A to tell you what kitchen tools you need

    B to tell you the steps to follow

    C to tell you the items you need for a recipe

    D to tell you the ways you can cook pizza

19. What is this selection mostly about?

    A how to make a pizza

    B why pizza makes a good breakfast

    C where pizzas come from

    D when to make pizzas

20. What is the main reason the author wrote this selection? Provide examples to support your response.

Name _____   Date _____

This selection describes how to make play dough at home. Read the selection. Then, answer the questions. On your answer sheet, darken the circle for each correct answer for multiple-choice items. For the open-ended item, write your answer on a separate sheet of paper.

Making Play Dough

Play dough is used by children to model interesting animals and objects. Play dough does not have to be bought in a store. Children can have fun making their own!

Follow the recipe to see how easy it is to make play dough.

3 cups flour   1 cup water

¼ cup salt   1 tablespoon vegetable oil

Mix the salt and flour together. Gradually add oil and water. Mix with hands until dough is well blended. Divide dough into 2 or 3 parts and mix a few drops of food coloring into each part. Store dough in an airtight container for up to one week. Have fun playing with it!

21. What reason does the author give for children to make their own play dough?

   A It is expensive to buy.

   B It lasts for a week.

   C It is not always available in stores.

   D It is fun to make.

22. What can you tell about the ingredients used to make play dough?

   A They are not safe to eat.

   B They are things many people have at home.

   C They spoil if they are not stored in an airtight container.

   D They are difficult to find in a store.

23. Which step should you do first when making play dough?

   A add food coloring to the mixture

   B divide the dough into parts

   C mix the dry ingredients together

   D mix the oil and water together

24. What can you tell about play dough based on the picture included with the selection?

   A It is very messy when children play with it.

   B It is difficult to work with.

   C It can be worked into many shapes.

   D It is more fun than other kinds of toys.

25. Which statement is the **best** summary of the selection?

   A It is easy to make your own play dough at home by mixing together several common ingredients.

   B When you make play dough, adding some food coloring will make the dough more interesting.

   C Children can make many different animals and other shapes with play dough.

   D You can use flour, salt, water, vegetable oil, and food coloring to make play dough.

26. Why do young children probably enjoy making play dough? Support your answer.

Language Arts and
Vocabulary Test Tips
and Practice

Standardized Tests for Language Arts

In the Language Arts Practice section, you will review common skills and terms that will help you answer language arts test questions. You will then answer multiple-choice questions that test how well you know grammar, usage, mechanics, and writing conventions. The multiple-choice questions for language arts will involve editing and revising items. There will also be some questions that are not multiple choice. For these questions, you will need to rewrite a sentence correctly.

Passage-Based Items

Some of the questions will be based on a passage. Other items will stand on their own. In some passages, words, phrases, or sentences might be underlined. These are the sections that the questions will ask about. In other passages, there might be blank lines. You will choose the word or words that best complete these sentences.

As you read a passage, pay attention to anything that looks or sounds incorrect. This might be a misspelled word, an incorrect verb, or words that do not agree in tense or number. You may want to mark things that seem like an error as you read.

Test Tips for Grammar and Usage

Complete Sentences

A complete sentence has a subject and a predicate. If a sentence is missing either part, it is a fragment.

Fragment: Flowers of all kinds in the garden.

Complete Sentence: Flowers of all kinds grow in the garden.

A run-on sentence has two or more parts, but the parts are joined incorrectly. To fix a run-on sentence, you can break it into two smaller sentences, add or change punctuation, or rearrange words in the sentence.

Run-on Sentence: The game is difficult to play, I don't understand the rules.

Correct: The game is difficult to play. I don't understand the rules.

Correct: The game is difficult to play because I don't understand the rules.

Correct: The game is difficult to play; I don't understand the rules.

Nouns and Pronouns

A noun names a person, place, thing, or idea.

> **Zach** loves watching **birds** in his **backyard** and plans to study **nature** in **college**.

A pronoun is used in place of one or more nouns.

> Darlene paints pictures of landscapes. Then, **she** hangs **them** in **her** house.

Verbs

A verb expresses action or a state of being.

> Randall **practiced** shooting the basketball every day. He **was** happy with the results.

Adjectives and Adverbs

An adjective describes a noun or a pronoun. Adjectives tell *what kind*, *which one*, *how much*, or *how many*. *A*, *an*, and *the* are special adjectives called articles.

> Jessica had **a good** idea about how to solve **the difficult** problem.

An adverb modifies a verb, an adjective, or another adverb. Adverbs tell *where*, *when*, *how*, or *to what extent*. Many adverbs end in *-ly*.

> **Yesterday**, Steve walked **quickly** toward his house because he wanted to show his parents how **well** he had done on his test.

Subject-Verb Agreement

Singular subjects take singular verbs. Use singular verbs for *each, either, neither, one, everyone, everybody, nobody, no one, anyone, someone,* or *somebody*.

> **Emily likes** playing soccer.
> **Each** of the students **brings** his or her lunch from home.
> **Neither** of the lamps **has** a bulb.
> **Everyone** in the class **likes** to read.

Plural subjects take plural verbs. Use plural verbs for *both, few, many,* or *several*.

> My **brothers are** good at sports.
> **Few** people **dislike** chocolate.
> **Many** of the students **have** pets.

Pronoun-Antecedent Agreement

A pronoun refers to a noun or another pronoun, called its antecedent. A pronoun should agree in number and gender with its antecedent.

> When **Tara** went to the store, **she** bought fabric for **her** quilt.
> **Mark and I** visited **our** grandparents when **we** went to the city.

Use singular pronouns to refer to *each, either, neither, one, everyone, everybody, no one, anyone, someone,* or *somebody*.

> **Each** boy on the team put on **his** uniform before **he** came to the game.
> **One** of the girls left **her** backpack at school.
> **Somebody** left **his** shoes in the boys' locker room.

Use plural pronouns to refer to *both, few, many,* or *several*.

> **Both** of my parents love **their** jobs.
> We liked **several** of the movies because **they** were funny.

Frequently Confused Words

Many words in English have similar or the same pronunciations but different spellings, meanings, and uses. Think about the correct spelling and usage of words you see in test items. The following are some examples of frequently confused words.

accept, except	bare, bear	chose, choose	hear, here
hole, whole	its, it's	knew, new	loose, lose
mail, male	meat, meet	passed, past	plain, plane
right, write	tail, tale	than, then	their, they're, there
threw, through	to, too, two	wear, where	your, you're

Test Tips for Mechanics

Capitalization

Capitalize the first word in every sentence.

> The cat loves to hide under the bed and swat at the dog.

Capitalize the pronoun *I*.

> When I got up this morning, I called my sister.

Capitalize proper nouns.

> On April 27, Claire will celebrate her birthday. She will have a party at Quarry Lake in Bellville.

Capitalize the first word and all important words in the title of a work such as a book, magazine, or TV show.

> Our teacher read a poem called "The Top of the Mountain."

Capitalize personal titles used with names of people.

> Ms. Wilson met President Obama.

Punctuation

End marks

Use a period at the end of a statement or request.

> Ellen adopted a dog from the animal shelter.
> Please lock the door when you go.

Use a question mark at the end of a question.

> When did the Civil War take place?

Use an exclamation point at the end of an exclamation or command.

> Look! There's a skunk in the bushes!
> Watch out for the puddle!

Commas

Use commas to separate items in a series.

> The cafeteria has bananas, oranges, and apples for sale.

Use commas before the conjunctions *and, but, or, nor, for, so,* or *yet* when the conjunction joins the parts of a compound sentence.

> Brian cooked pizza for dinner, and Nikki made a delicious salad.

Use commas to set off interrupters.

> Lisa, my older sister, loves to pick flowers and arrange them in vases.
>
> No, I've never been to a hockey game.
>
> Mark, however, loved the winter weather.

Use commas to separate items in dates and addresses.

> My baby brother was born on Wednesday, July 11, 2012.
>
> You can send a letter to the president at 1600 Pennsylvania Avenue NW, Washington, DC 20500.

Use a comma after the opening of a friendly letter and after the closing of any letter.

> Dear Aunt Kelly,
>
> Sincerely,

Apostrophes

Use apostrophes to form possessives. To form a singular possessive, use an apostrophe and *s* at the end of a noun.

> the cat's toys   my best friend's house   Evan's job

To form a plural possessive of a word ending in *s*, add an apostrophe at the end. If the plural noun does not end in *s*, add an apostrophe and *s*.

> the cars' horns   the trees' leaves   the children's books

Use apostrophes to form contractions. The apostrophe takes the place of the letters that have been removed.

> she is   she's   have not   haven't
>
> I have   I've   you are   you're

Spelling

A few common spelling rules can help you figure out if words are misspelled. Remember that there are always exceptions to the rules for spelling English words.

Silent *e*

In a word that ends with a silent *e*, remember to drop the *e* before adding an ending that starts with a vowel.

> make   making   believe   believable   hope   hopeful

Double a Final Consonant

In words that end with a short vowel and a consonant, the consonant is usually doubled before an ending that starts with a vowel.

admit   admitted   pop   popping   hot   hottest

i Before *e*

When spelling words, use *i* before *e*, except after *c* and in words that sound like *weigh*.

piece   chief   neighbor   deceive

Language Arts Practice

Choose the correct word or words to complete each sentence. On your answer sheet, darken the circle for each correct answer for multiple-choice items. For the short-answer item, write your answer on a separate sheet of paper.

Although geckos are small lizards, not plants, (1) grow buds after they shed their tails. Geckos can shed their tails when they (2) by another animal. When a gecko's tail drops off, it continues to wriggle on the ground. The attacker (3) be confused by the wriggling tail. This gives the gecko time to escape. Soon, new cells grow in the place where the old tail had been. These cells are called buds. It takes about eight to twelve months (4) a gecko to grow a (5) full-sized tail.

1. What word should fill in blank 1?

   A it

   B they

   C their

   D its

2. Using the correct form of the verb "to attack," rewrite the second sentence (sentence with blank 2).

3. What word or words should fill in blank 3?

   A can

   B ought to

   C should

   D must

4. What word should fill in blank 4?

   A around

   B from

   C for

   D in

5. What word or words should fill in blank 5?

   A newly

   B newest

   C new

   D more new

Name _____ Date _____

Choose the correct word or words to complete each sentence. On your answer sheet, darken the circle for each correct answer for multiple-choice items. For the short-answer item, write your answer on a separate sheet of paper.

> Have you ever (6) a dog sing? They may not actually sing, but dogs, wolves, and coyotes (7) make a kind of music. They howl. Why do they do it? Scientists have (8) ideas about why these members of the dog family (9). They believe that howling is a way for the animals to communicate. Some scientists think that wolves usually howl to call back members (10) the pack that have wandered away.

6. Using the correct form of the verb "to hear," rewrite the first sentence (sentence with blank 6).

7. What word should fill in blank 7?

   A due

   B dew

   C do

   D doo

8. What words should fill in blank 8?

   A different few

   B different many

   C no different

   D several different

9. What word or words should fill in blank 9?

   A howl

   B make noise

   C talk

   D whisper

10. What word should fill in blank 10?

    A against

    B on

    C along

    D of

Name _____ Date _____

Choose the word or words that best complete each sentence. On your answer sheet, darken the circle for each correct answer.

11. The _____ about 5,000 feet in the air.

    A plane flies

    B plane fly

    C planes flys

    D planes flies

12. The theater asks people _____ use their cell phones during the movie to leave.

    A which

    B who

    C what

    D whose

13. The coyote dug _____ den under a large rock in the park.

    A it's

    B its'

    C its

    D it

14. We _____ TV when the phone rang.

    A will be watching

    B were watch

    C watching

    D were watching

15. The mother birds feed _____ babies insects.

    A there

    B they're

    C their

    D there're

16. Bella hurt her hand last week, and now she can't practice the piano _____ more.

    A any

    B no

    C some

    D none

Read each question and choose the best answer. On your answer sheet, darken the circle for each correct answer.

17. Choose the word that **best** completes the paragraph.

> Marie was digging a new flower bed outside the house. Suddenly, her shovel made a pinging sound. Before Marie knew what had happened, a fountain of water _____ from the ground, soaking Marie with its spray. She dashed to turn off the water.

A dripped

B gushed

C came

D leaked

18. Find the sentence that **best** combines the following sentences.

> Her heart was pounding. She started to creep down the staircase.

A Although she started to creep down the staircase, her heart was pounding.

B Down the staircase, her heart was pounding as she started to creep.

C She started to creep with a pounding heart, down the staircase.

D With her heart pounding, she started to creep down the staircase.

19. Find the sentence that is complete and is written correctly.

A A watershed is an area of land, it collects water that falls as rain and snow.

B As rain and snow fall to Earth and collect in the watershed.

C Rain and snow fall and are collected in an area of land called a watershed.

D Is the area in which rain and snow fall to Earth.

20. Read these sentences. Which sentence should be revised to make the language more formal?

> (1) Popcorn can be a healthful snack when it is prepared properly. (2) It tastes really yummy, too. (3) To make healthful popcorn, use an air popper instead of oil. (4) Also limit the amount of butter and salt you add.

A Sentence 1

B Sentence 2

C Sentence 3

D Sentence 4

Identify the type of error, if any, in each underlined section. On your answer sheet, darken the circle for each correct answer for multiple-choice items. For the short-answer item, write your answer on a separate sheet of paper.

Who could ever forget the terrible sandstorm <u>we had last March.</u>
                                                                    21

It was one of the most frightening <u>expereinces of my life!</u> For many
                                                                    22

months, there had been almost no rain. <u>December January and</u>
                                                                    23

<u>February had been especially dry.</u> No rain fell <u>in March either but the</u>
                                                                    24

wind blew constantly. On many days the sky was more brown than

<u>blue, because, the air was so filled with sand.</u>
25

21. What is the error in underlined section 21?

   A Spelling

   B Capitalization

   C Punctuation

   D No Error

22. What is the error in underlined section 22?

   A Spelling

   B Capitalization

   C Punctuation

   D No Error

23. Rewrite the third sentence correctly
    (underlined section 23).

24. What is the error in underlined section 24?

   A Spelling

   B Capitalization

   C Punctuation

   D No Error

25. What is the error in underlined section 25?

   A Spelling

   B Capitalization

   C Punctuation

   D No Error

Identify the type of error, if any, in each underlined section. On your answer sheet, darken the circle for each correct answer for multiple-choice items. For the short-answer item, write your answer on a separate sheet of paper.

Linda got her first <u>puppy on June 1 2001</u>. Her family picked it up at
                         26

a farm <u>in Ames, iowa. Linda</u> had waited a long time to get the
            27

puppy. First she read a book called *Caring for Your New Dog*. <u>Then</u>
                                         28

<u>she talked to a dog trainner</u> to learn what to expect. <u>"Hooray! Linda</u>
                                         29

<u>shouted</u> when she saw the new puppy. "I can't wait to take you

<u>home!" Lindas new puppy liked her, too.</u>
    30

26. What is the error in underlined section 26?

  A Spelling

  B Capitalization

  C Punctuation

  D No Error

27. What is the error in underlined section 27?

  A Spelling

  B Capitalization

  C Punctuation

  D No Error

28. What is the error in underlined section 28?

  A Spelling

  B Capitalization

  C Punctuation

  D No Error

29. What is the error in underlined section 29?

  A Spelling

  B Capitalization

  C Punctuation

  D No Error

30. Rewrite the last sentence correctly (underlined section 30).

Name _____   Date _____

Read each question and choose the best answer. On your answer sheet, darken the circle for each correct answer.

31. Choose the sentence that shows the capital letters used correctly.

    A Canoe Cove is a village on Prince Edward Island, canada.

    B Canoe Cove is a village on Prince Edward Island, Canada.

    C Canoe Cove is a Village on Prince Edward Island, Canada.

    D Canoe cove is a village on prince Edward island, Canada.

32. Choose the answer that shows the **correct** punctuation.

    A Julia asked, "Who wants to play chess?"

    B Julia "asked, Who wants to play chess?"

    C "Julia asked, Who wants to play chess?"

    D Julia asked, "Who wants to play chess?

33. Choose the sentence that is correct.

    A Marco will celebrate his tenth birthday, on, August 3, 2015.

    B Marco will celebrate his tenth birthday on August 3, 2015.

    C Marco will celebrate his tenth birthday on August 3 2015.

    D marco will celebrate his tenth birthday on august 3, 2015.

34. Choose the correct word to complete the sentence.

> The house is _____ by tall trees.

    A serrounded

    B surounded

    C surroundded

    D surrounded

35. Choose the correct word to complete the sentence.

> Emma _____ the alphabet when she was four years old.

    A learned

    B lurned

    C learnt

    D learened

Read each question and choose the best answer. On your answer sheet, darken the circle for each correct answer.

36. Choose the sentence that shows the **correct** punctuation.

   A Has Mrs Robson ever visited Philadelphia Pennsylvania?

   B Has Mrs. Robson ever visited Philadelphia, Pennsylvania?

   C Has Mrs. Robson ever visited Philadelphia, Pennsylvania.

   D Has Mrs. Robson, ever visited Philadelphia, Pennsylvania!

37. Choose the answer that shows the **correct** punctuation.

   A At the scout troop meeting next week we will serve salad, pizza, and chicken, sandwiches.

   B At the scout troop meeting, next week, we will serve salad pizza, and chicken sandwiches.

   C At the scout troop meeting next week, we will serve salad, pizza, and chicken sandwiches.

   D At the scout troop meeting next week we will serve salad pizza and chicken sandwiches.

38. Choose the sentence that is correct.

   A Did you enjoy the mexican food they served at the Party?

   B Did you enjoy, the Mexican food they served, at the party.

   C Did you enjoy the Mexican Food they served at the party.

   D Did you enjoy the Mexican food they served at the party?

39. Choose the correct word to complete the sentence.

   Lakshmi is _____ a letter.

   A writing

   B writeing

   C writting

   D riting

40. Choose the sentence that is correct.

   A Oh, said Beryl, "I give up!"

   B "Oh," said Beryl, I give up!

   C "Oh," said Beryl, "I give up!"

   D "Oh, said Beryl, I give up!"

Standardized Tests for Vocabulary

In the Vocabulary Practice section, you will review common skills and terms and learn strategies for answering vocabulary questions. Then, you will answer multiple-choice questions for vocabulary that ask you to identify the correct meaning of words using context clues; use prefixes, suffixes, and roots; and analyze the relationships between words.

Test Tips for Vocabulary

Using Context Clues

One way to find the meaning of an unfamiliar word is to look for context clues in nearby phrases and sentences. Follow these steps:

Step 1: Look at the context of the unfamiliar word. See if the words and sentences around it provide clues to the word's meaning.
- Look for definitions, synonyms, or antonyms that give clues to the unfamiliar word.
- Look at how the word is used in the sentence. Determine the part of speech.

Step 2: Use the context clues to guess the unfamiliar word's meaning.

Step 3: Check your definition by inserting it in the selection in place of the unfamiliar word. Remember that your definition should be the same part of speech as the unfamiliar word.

Understanding Word Relationships

Analogies are relationships between words. You may be asked to complete analogies on standardized tests.

oak : tree = sparrow : _____

A maple   **B** pine   **C** spider   **D** bird

Follow these steps to complete an analogy.

Step 1: Read the first two words. Notice what part of speech they are. In the example, oak and tree are both nouns.

Step 2: Figure out how the first two words are related. In the example, an oak is a type of tree.

Step 3: Look at the third word. In the example, it is sparrow. Sparrow is also a noun. In an analogy, the third and fourth words should have the same relationship as the first and second words. This means you'd want to figure out what a sparrow is a type of.

Step 4: Look at the answer choices. Maple and pine are types of trees. They're not correct. A sparrow is not a type of spider. A sparrow is a type of bird. The word bird belongs in the blank. Oak is a type of tree, and sparrow is a type of bird.

Using Word Parts

Many words are made up of various word parts. The **root** of a word is the part that carries the word's core meaning. Many roots of English words come from Latin and Greek. Knowing the meanings of these roots can help you figure out an unfamiliar word. A **prefix** is added to the beginning of a word to create a new word. A **suffix** is added to the end of a word to create a new word.

Common Roots

Root	Meaning	Example
micro	small	microscope, microwave
trans	across	transportation, transfer
tele	far off	television, telescope
vid, vis	see	video, visual
geo	earth	geography, geology

Common Prefixes

Prefix	Meaning	Example
dis-	not	discontinue
pre-	before	preheat
re-	again	resell
un-	not	unlike
mis-	wrongly	misunderstand
in-/im-/ir-	not	impossible, inability

Common Suffixes

Suffix	Meaning	Example
-ful	full of	hopeful
-less	without	seedless
-ness	state of being	kindness
-ion/-tion	act, process	action, location
-ly	characteristic of	happily

Identifying Antonyms and Synonyms

Antonyms are words that are opposite in meaning.

loud / quiet
frozen / boiling

Synonyms are words with the same or nearly the same meaning.

dull / boring
yell / scream

Analyzing Multiple-Meaning Words

Some words have more than one meaning and can function as different parts of speech. To choose the correct meaning of a multiple-meaning word, determine what part of speech it is. Then, look at its context, the words and sentences around it.

> Each girl wrote her name on a **slip** of paper. (meaning: "a small piece")
> You can easily **slip** on an icy sidewalk. (meaning: "to fall")

Use these steps to decide on the correct meaning of a multiple-meaning word:

Step 1: Decide what part of speech it is.

Step 2: Look at its context, the words and sentences around it.

Step 3: Check your definition against the original sentence to see if it makes sense.

Analyzing Connotations and Denotations

The denotation of a word is its dictionary meaning. Connotations are the feelings and ideas that have become attached to certain words. A word's connotations can be positive or negative. A word with positive connotations makes you think of good things. A word with negative connotations makes you think of bad or unpleasant things.

As you read, think about the word choices an author makes. Do the words make you think of something positive or negative? Compare the connotations in these sentences.

> The cook wore sloppy clothing.
> The chef dressed in casual clothing.

Idioms, Adages, and Proverbs

The words in an idiom have a different meaning than their dictionary definition. To figure out the meaning of an idiom, think about the context and look for clues.

> Ana thought her math test was a piece of cake.

In this sentence, the math test is not a kind of food. The idiom *piece of cake* instead means "easy."

Adages and proverbs are traditional sayings that people accept as true. Often these sayings contain some truth, wisdom, or insight about people's behavior.

> History repeats itself.
> A fool and his money are soon parted.
> The early bird catches the worm.

Name _____   Date _____

Vocabulary Practice

Read the selection below. Then, answer the questions. On your answer sheet, darken the circle for each correct answer.

Mathew Brady was a renowned photographer in the 1800s. He opened a New York photography studio in 1844 and became well known for his portraits of famous people. When the Civil War erupted in the 1860s, he left his successful studio to work in the battlefields. There, he captured the misery and cruelty of war through the eye of his camera. People were shocked and upset by what the images showed about war.

By taking pictures that showed the horror of war, Brady set the stage for today's photojournalists. To record history, people in this profession face all kinds of dangerous situations. As part of their daily work, they may face unsafe situations, bad weather, crowds, and other obstacles in order to photograph the world's events.

1. Which word or words in the selection mean **about the same** as renowned?

   A opened

   B well known

   C portraits

   D successful

2. What does the word erupted mean in this selection?

   A broke out suddenly

   B came to an end

   C paused for a while

   D started slowly

3. What does the phrase <u>eye of his camera</u> mean in this selection?

   A The camera blinked like an eye when it took a picture.

   B The camera had a lens that he could see through.

   C The camera was something he could look at.

   D The camera saw by capturing an image like an eye does.

4. What is the meaning of the phrase <u>set the stage</u> in this selection?

   A built a place to put on a play

   B provided a way of doing things

   C did an acting job

   D paused during a long trip

5. What do <u>photojournalists</u> most likely do?

   A study pictures

   B write in a diary every day

   C tell a news story through pictures

   D use a movie camera to make films

6. What is a <u>profession</u>?

   A a payment

   B an event

   C a job

   D an image

7. Based on clues in the selection, you can tell that <u>obstacles</u> are

   A rewards for completing a job.

   B people who are difficult to work with.

   C unusual events in a faraway place.

   D difficult things you must get around.

On your answer sheet, darken the circle for each correct answer.

8. Choose the word that means the **same** or **almost the same** as the underlined word.

> Rice farmers irrigate their crops.

A plow

B plant

C harvest

D water

9. Choose the word that means the **same** or **almost the same** as the underlined word.

> It is essential that you follow the directions carefully.

A necessary

B usual

C told

D great

10. Choose the word that **best** completes the blank.

> Fingers are to hands as toes are to _____.

A shoes

B gloves

C feet

D thumbs

11. Read these sentences. Choose the word that **best** completes **both** sentences.

> Pepe was _____ at the concert.
> We bought a pretty _____ for Gloria.

A not

B ribbon

C present

D picture

Answer the questions. On your answer sheet, darken the circle for each correct answer.

12. Read these sentences. Choose the word that **best** completes **both** sentences.

> I just had a _____ dinner.
> Please turn off the _____ in the kitchen.

A small

B great

C light

D blender

13. Read these sentences. What word or words help you figure out the meaning of the word accelerated?

> Mrs. Brown accelerated so that she would make the green light. She sped up to thirty miles per hour.

A make

B green

C sped up

D per hour

14. Native Americans thought that buffaloes were very _____ animals. The meat was used for food, and the hides were used for clothing and tents.

A useless

B useful

C misused

D unused

15. Read this dictionary entry for the word mean.

> **mean (mēn)**
> 1 *verb*   to signify or represent
> 2 *verb*   to intend
> 3 *noun*   in math, the average value of a set of numbers
> 4 *adjective* unkind

Which definition matches how mean is used in this sentence?

> I did not mean to hurt your feelings.

A Definition 1

B Definition 2

C Definition 3

D Definition 4

Writing Test Tips and Practice

Standardized Tests for Writing

In the Writing Practice section, you will read general strategies for answering writing prompts and review graphic organizers that can help you plan your writing. Then, you will learn about responding to three different types of writing prompts: opinion, informative, and narrative. Standardized tests for writing test your ability in five areas of writing: focus, content, organization, style, and conventions.

Scoring the Writing Prompts

Your response to the writing prompts will be scored on a 4-point scale or a 6-point scale depending on your parent's or teacher's preference. The response will be scored for both composition (focus, content, organization, and style) and conventions. If a response cannot be read, makes no sense, has too little information to be scored, or is blank, it will not receive a composition score. A response that is off-topic also will not receive a composition score. However, an off-topic response will receive a conventions score.

SCORING ON A 4-POINT SCALE:

A *4-point* response demonstrates **advanced** success with the writing task. The essay:

- focuses consistently on a clear and reasonable thesis or position

- shows effective organization throughout, with smooth transitions

- offers thoughtful, creative ideas and reasons

- develops ideas or supports a position thoroughly, using examples; details; convincing, fully elaborated explanations; or reasons and evidence

- exhibits mature control of written language

A *3-point* response demonstrates **competent** success with the writing task. In general, the essay:
- focuses on a clear thesis or reasonable position, with minor distractions

- shows effective organization, with minor lapses

- offers mostly thoughtful ideas and reasons

- develops ideas adequately and elaborates reasons and evidence with a mixture of the general and the specific

- exhibits general control of written language

A *2-point* response demonstrates **limited** success with the writing task. The essay may:
- include some loosely related ideas that distract from the writer's focus or position
- show some organization, with noticeable gaps in the logical flow of ideas
- offer routine, predictable ideas and reasons
- develop or support ideas with uneven elaboration and reasoning
- exhibit limited control of written language

A *1-point* response demonstrates **emerging** effort with the writing task. In general, the essay:
- shows little awareness of the topic and purpose for writing
- lacks organization
- offers unclear and confusing ideas
- develops ideas in a minimal way, if at all, or shows minimal reasoning or elaboration
- exhibits major problems with control of written language

SCORING ON A 6-POINT SCALE:

A *6-point* response demonstrates **advanced** success with the writing task. The essay:
- focuses consistently on a clear and reasonable thesis or position
- shows effective organization throughout, with smooth transitions
- offers thoughtful, creative ideas and reasons
- supports a position thoroughly, using convincing, fully elaborated reasons and evidence
- exhibits mature control of written language

A *5-point* response demonstrates **proficient** success with the writing task. In general, the essay:
- focuses on a clear and reasonable thesis or position
- shows effective organization, with transitions
- offers thoughtful ideas and reasons
- supports a position competently, using convincing, well-elaborated reasons and evidence
- exhibits sufficient control of written language

A *4-point* response demonstrates **competent** success with the writing task. In general, the essay:

- focuses on a reasonable thesis or position, with minor distractions

- shows effective organization, with minor lapses

- offers mostly thoughtful ideas and reasons

- elaborates reasons and evidence with a mixture of the general and the specific

- exhibits general control of written language

A *3-point* response demonstrates **limited** success with the writing task. The essay may:

- include some loosely related ideas that distract from the writer's thesis or position

- show some organization, with noticeable gaps in the logical flow of ideas

- offer routine, predictable ideas and reasons

- support ideas with uneven reasoning and elaboration

- exhibit limited control of written language

A *2-point* response demonstrates **basic** success with the writing task. In general, the essay:

- includes loosely related ideas that seriously distract from the writer's purpose

- shows minimal organization, with major gaps in the logical flow of ideas

- offers ideas and reasons that merely skim the surface

- supports ideas with inadequate reasoning and elaboration

- exhibits significant problems with control of written language

A *1-point* response demonstrates **emerging** effort with the writing task. In general, the essay:

- shows little awareness of the topic and purpose for writing

- lacks organization

- offers unclear and confusing ideas

- demonstrates minimal reasoning or elaboration

- exhibits major problems with control of written language

Test Tips for Responding to a Prompt

- **First, read the prompt carefully.** Be sure that you understand exactly what the prompt is asking.

- **Decide what kind of response you are being asked to write.** Ask yourself, "What is the purpose of this response?" A persuasive writing prompt asks you to give your opinion about something. A narrative prompt asks you to tell a story. An informative prompt asks you to give information about a topic.

- **Many tests are timed. Before you begin writing, consider how much time you have.** Allow about one-third of the time to prewrite and plan your essay. Allow about one-third of the time to write a first draft. Finally, allow about one-third of the time to edit the first draft and write a final version. As you practice planning, prewriting, and writing, note how much time you spend doing each of these things. This will help you have a better idea of how much time to allow for each task. Remember that the time you spend planning and prewriting makes the job of writing much easier.

- **Next, organize your thoughts.** Write notes on a separate sheet of paper before you write your response. First, determine the main point of your response. Your thesis sentence, or the statement of your main point, should include the general topic, as well as the main idea. It should set the tone and catch your reader's attention. Most importantly, it should answer the prompt. This will be the anchor to your response. Then, come up with ideas to support your thesis sentence. Your ideas should include the major points that you want to cover. Different graphic organizers can help you develop and organize the points in your essay.

- **Write in complete sentences.** Your sentences and paragraphs should flow smoothly. Your sentences should support the main idea and should be arranged in an order that makes sense to the reader. Be as specific as possible when stating your ideas. Make use of transitional words or phrases like *also*, *however*, or *finally*. Also, remember to write neatly.

- **Finally, proofread your response.** Check for spelling and punctuation errors. Look for run-on sentences and sentence fragments. Check verb tenses to see if you have used them correctly. Make the necessary edits as neat as possible.

If you follow these guidelines, you should do well on the writing section of standardized tests. Remember that practice makes perfect. Read and write as often as possible about whatever subjects you prefer, and you will see that writing responses will eventually come quite naturally.

Graphic Organizers for Writing

Brainstorming Significant Details

A word web can help you identify details about your topic. Write your topic in the middle circle. Then, write words or phrases that come to mind in the outer circles.

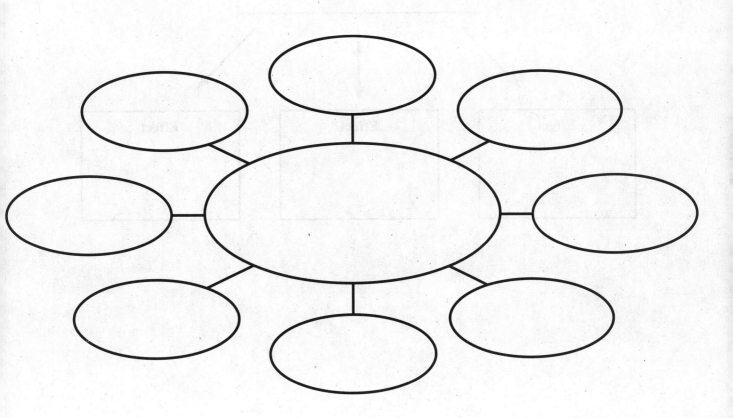

Cause-and-Effect Chart

You can use a cause and effect chart to show the reasons something happened (the causes) or the results of an event (the effects).

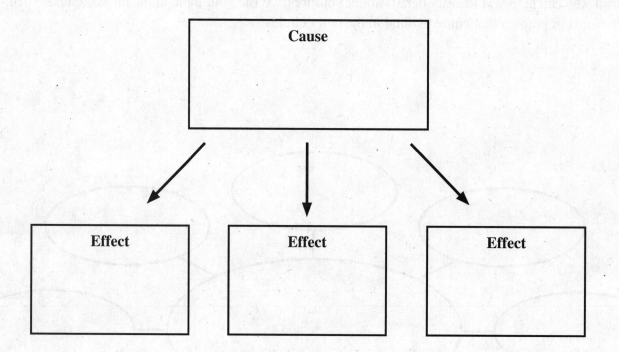

Sequence of Events

A sequence chart is useful if you are writing a narrative that includes different events. The sequence chart can help you identify events and put them in the correct time order.

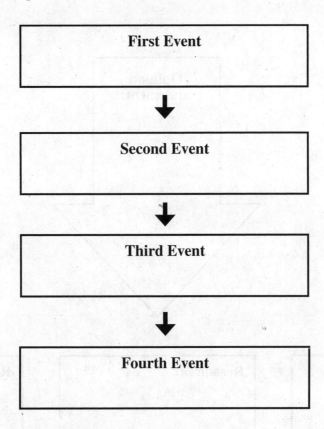

First Event

↓

Second Event

↓

Third Event

↓

Fourth Event

Main Idea and Details

A main idea and detail chart can help you identify your thesis sentence and come up with details that support it.

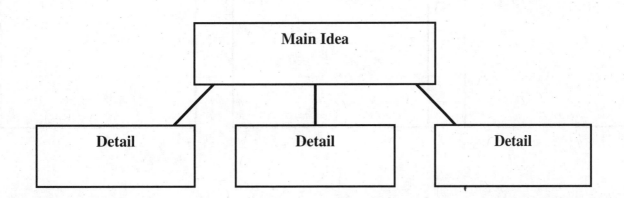

Main Idea

Detail   **Detail**   **Detail**

Persuasion

If you need to persuade your reader, you might want to use this organizer. Write your opinion in the arrow at the top. Then, list convincing reasons and supporting details.

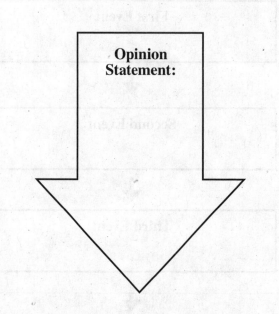

Opinion
Statement:

Reason 1:	Reason 2:	Reason 3:

Support:	Support:	Support:
1.	1.	1.
2.	2.	2.

Writing Prompt 1: Opinion

Plan, write, and proofread an opinion letter in response to the writing prompt below.

> If you could change one rule that you must currently follow, what rule would you change? How would you change it? Write an opinion letter to your parent, coach, or whoever enforces the rule. Describe the rule and explain how it should be changed. Give reasons and information to support your opinion.

As you write your letter, be sure to

- Focus on one rule that you want to change.

- Explain why you think the rule should be changed.

- Describe how you would change the rule.

- Explain the reasons changing the rule would be good.

- Organize your opinion letter so that your ideas have a logical order.

- Keep your audience in mind as you write.

- Edit your letter for correct grammar and usage.

Prewriting

1. **Analyze the Prompt.** Read the prompt carefully to identify the purpose of and the audience for your response.

Purpose

The prompt asks you to name a rule that you would change. Then, you will write an opinion letter to the person who enforces the rule explaining how you would change the rule. Your letter should give reasons and information that support your opinion.

Complete the following sentence:

My purpose is to convince _____ to change _____.

Audience

According to the prompt, who is your audience? Use the following step-by-step method to analyze the audience identified in the prompt.

Steps	Explanation	Your Response
Step 1 Ask yourself, "Who is the audience for this letter?"	Look at the prompt. Who will read your letter?	
Step 2 Ask, "How does my audience feel about rules? How will my audience feel about changing a rule?"	Think about why this rule exists. How could the rule be improved?	
Step 3 Ask, "How can I get my audience to agree with me? What kinds of reasons will convince my audience?"	Help your reader understand the problems with the rule. Why are your changes to the rule a good idea?	
Step 4 Ask, "How should I address my audience in the letter? What kind of tone and language should I use?"	Think about the correct way to write to an adult. For example, how should you address the letter? Should you use formal or informal language?	

64

2. **Brainstorm Ideas.** Use the graphic organizer below to help identify rules. Choosing an idea that you believe in will greatly improve your writing and your ability to support your opinion.

Rule	Good or Bad?	Why?

Name _____ Date _____

3. Develop Your Idea. Identify the rule that you would like to change. Then, identify what is wrong with the rule. What problems does it cause? How will your change to the rule be better?

Use a web graphic organizer to brainstorm details about the rule and how you will change it. Write the name of the rule in the center oval. Then, write details in the outer ovals.

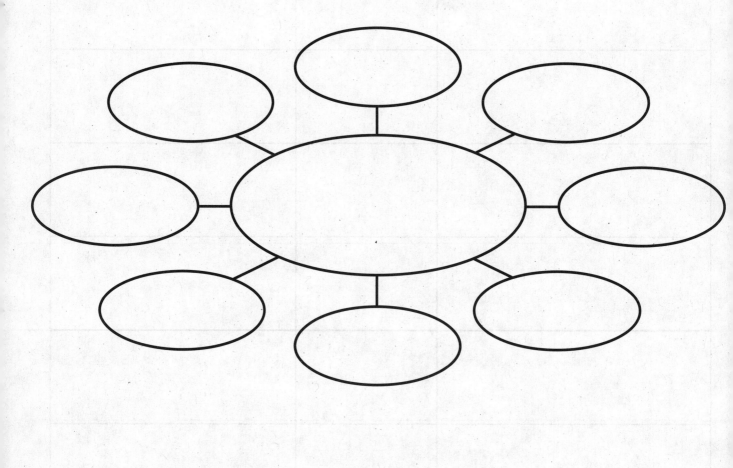

4. **Organize Your Ideas.** Now that you have brainstormed details, organize your thoughts in a way that makes sense. In the organizer below, write a sentence identifying the rule that you want to change. Then, add the reasons that support changing the rule. Use the information that you brainstormed on the previous page to decide on your strongest reasons. Finally, add details that support these reasons.

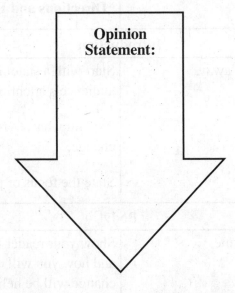

Opinion Statement:

Reason 1:	Reason 2:	Reason 3:

Support:	Support:	Support:
1.	1.	1.
2.	2.	2.

Drafting Your Response

Use the following framework to draft your response to the opinion prompt. Write your draft on your own paper.

Framework	Directions and Explanations
Introduction	
Get your audience interested right away.	Start with a statement or question that grabs your audience's attention.
Give background information.	Explain what's wrong with the rule you want to change.
Include a clear thesis sentence.	State the focus or point of your letter.
Body	
Explain how you will change the rule.	Show your reader how you will improve the rule and how you will change it. Explain how the change will be helpful.
Give reasons and information for support.	Present your ideas. You can organize your supporting reasons for changing the rule by starting with the strongest reason first.
Present your ideas in a logical order.	Remember to start a new paragraph when you develop a new reason.
Conclusion	
Remind your audience why you want to change the rule and how it will make things better.	Restate your thesis sentence. Remind your audience what is wrong with the old rule and how the new rule will be an improvement.

Name _____ Date _____

Evaluating, Revising, and Editing Your Response

Use the following strategies to evaluate and revise your response. You may make your revisions directly on your first draft, or, if necessary, write your revised draft on your own paper.

Evaluation Guidelines for Opinion Essay		
Evaluation Questions	**Tips**	**Revision Techniques**
1. Does the opinion letter have a clear thesis that addresses the prompt?	Ask, "Does my response state an opinion about how a rule should be changed?"	If necessary, revise your thesis so that it addresses the prompt.
2. Is the response organized appropriately?	Check for features of a letter, such as a greeting and closing.	If necessary, revise to make sure your response is in the form of a letter.
3. Does the response include reasons to support the opinion?	Put a checkmark next to each reason.	Support your ideas by explaining why the rule should be changed.
4. Are the reasons supported by facts and details?	Lightly underline facts and details that support the reasons.	Add examples or facts for support.
5. Are the opinion and reasons logically linked?	Look for connecting words and phrases like *for instance*, *in addition*, and *in order to*.	Add linking words to show how ideas are connected.
6. Does the response include a strong conclusion?	Check for a concluding paragraph. Does it restate your thesis?	Add a conclusion or revise so that the conclusion clearly states your thesis.

Proofing Your Response

Final Proofreading Guidelines

Proofread your response to ensure that it

- Contains only complete sentences and no fragments.
- Uses proper subject-verb agreement, pronoun agreement, and consistent verb tense.
- Uses correct capitalization, punctuation, and spelling.

Draft your final letter in the space below.

_____

_____

_____

_____

_____

_____

_____

_____

_____

_____

_____

_____

_____

_____

_____

_____

_____

_____

_____

_____

_____

Name _____ Date _____

_____
_____
_____
_____
_____
_____
_____
_____
_____
_____
_____
_____
_____
_____
_____
_____
_____
_____
_____
_____
_____
_____
_____
_____
_____
_____
_____
_____
_____
_____
_____

Writing Prompt 2: Informative

Plan, write, and proofread an informative essay in response to the writing prompt below.

> Write an essay for an adult about a holiday or celebration that is important to you or your family. Explain what the holiday or celebration is like and what makes it special.

As you write your essay, be sure to

- Focus on one holiday or celebration.

- Clearly state your main idea.

- Describe the special day in detail.

- Organize your writing and present your ideas in a logical order.

- Keep your audience in mind as you write.

- Edit your essay for correct grammar and usage.

Prewriting

1. **Analyze the Prompt.** Read the prompt carefully to identify the purpose of and the audience for your response.

Purpose

The prompt asks you to name a holiday or celebration that is important to you or your family. You will write an informative essay to explain why you like this holiday or celebration and why it is important to you. Your essay should include descriptive details to support your topic.

Complete the following sentence:
My purpose is to inform about _____ and explain _____.

Audience

According to the prompt, who is your audience? Use the following step-by-step method to analyze the audience identified in the prompt.

Steps	Explanation	Your Response
Step 1 Ask yourself, "Who is the audience for this letter?"	Look at the prompt. Who will read your essay?	
Step 2 Ask, "What will my audience already know about this holiday or celebration?"	Remember that your reader will want to know what makes this day special.	
Step 3 Ask, "What details will matter most to my audience?"	Think about what details you should include. You may not want to tell your audience every possible detail.	
Step 4 Ask, "How should I present the information in my essay?"	Remember that your reader is an adult. Think about the best way to write to an adult. Should your language be formal or informal?	

Name _____ Date _____

2. **Brainstorm Topic Ideas.** Use the graphic organizer below to help you identify holidays and celebrations, what you like about them, and why they are important. Choosing a topic that you care about will greatly improve your writing and your ability to describe it in detail.

Holiday or Celebration	What I Like About It	Why It's Important

3. **Develop Your Topic Idea.** Choose the holiday or celebration that you want to write about. Then, choose information about the holiday, including facts, details, and quotations. Think about when it takes place, how you celebrate it, and why it is important to your family.

Use a web graphic organizer to help you brainstorm details and information you want to include in your essay. Write the name of the holiday in the center oval. Then, write details in the outer ovals.

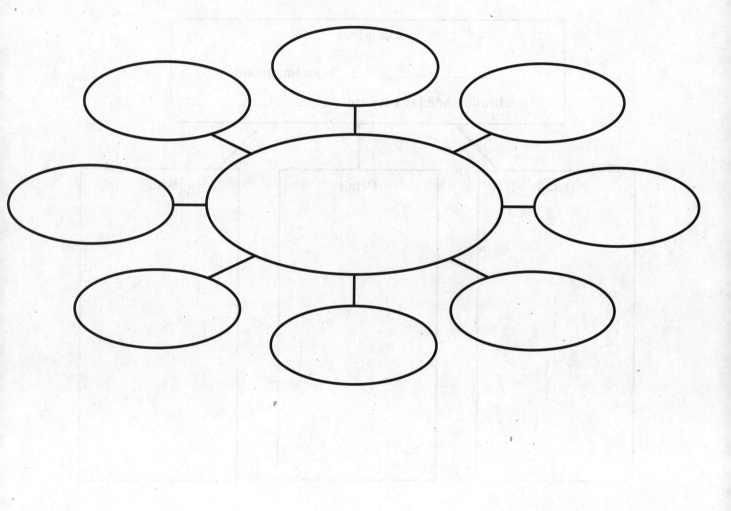

4. **Organize Your Ideas.** Now that you have brainstormed details, organize your thoughts in a way that makes sense. In the main idea organizer below, write a sentence describing the holiday or celebration you have chosen. Your main idea should explain why the celebration or holiday is important. Then, fill in the supporting details that explain what's important about the celebration or holiday. Use the details that you brainstormed on the previous page to help you. Remember that you can add more information to the details boxes.

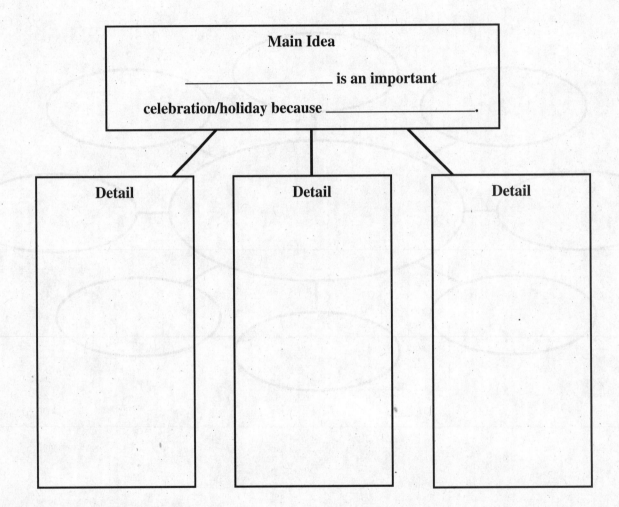

Drafting Your Response

Use the following framework to draft your response to the informative writing prompt. Write your draft on your own paper.

Framework	Directions and Explanations
Introduction	
Get your audience interested right away.	To get your audience interested, start with a statement or question that grabs the reader's attention.
Give background information.	Provide background on the holiday or celebration, such as what date or time of year it occurs.
Include a clear thesis sentence.	State the focus or point of your essay. Be sure you focus on only one celebration or holiday and that you state the focus.
Body	
Provide information that explains why the celebration or holiday is important.	Tell your reader why the celebration or holiday is significant.
Give facts and details for support.	Present your ideas. Develop each of your supporting details. Include sensory details about the celebration or holiday that help your reader picture it.
Present your ideas in a logical order.	Remember to start a new paragraph when you develop a new detail. Use connecting words to show how the ideas are related.
Conclusion	
Remind your audience why the celebration or holiday is important.	Restate your thesis sentence and sum up what's special about the celebration or holiday in your essay.

Evaluating, Revising, and Editing Your Response

Use the following strategies to evaluate and revise your response. You may make your revisions directly on your first draft, or, if necessary, write your revised draft on your own paper.

Evaluation Guidelines for Informative Essay		
Evaluation Questions	**Tips**	**Revision Techniques**
1. Does the informative essay have a clear thesis that addresses the prompt?	Ask, "Does my response focus on a single celebration or holiday? Does it explain why that day is special?"	If necessary, revise your thesis so that it addresses the prompt.
2. Is the response organized appropriately?	Check that paragraphs are developed and that each paragraph develops a separate detail.	If necessary, break your response into paragraphs and delete repeated information.
3. Do the details you included support the main idea and help the reader understand why the celebration or holiday is important?	Put a checkmark next to each supporting detail.	Cut out information that is unimportant or off-topic. Add more details if needed to explain your main idea.
4. Do you provide enough examples in your details?	Lightly underline facts, examples, and information.	Add more examples or facts for support.
5. Does the essay have a logical flow?	Look for connecting words and phrases like *another*, *for example*, *also*, and *because*.	Add linking words to show how ideas are connected.
6. Does the response use precise language and appropriate vocabulary?	Identify places where the writing is wordy.	Replace wordy phrases. Choose active verbs and precise words.
7. Does the response include a strong conclusion?	Check for a concluding paragraph. Does it restate your thesis?	Add a conclusion or revise so that the conclusion clearly states your thesis.

Proofing Your Response

Final Proofreading Guidelines

Proofread your response to ensure that it

- Contains only complete sentences and no fragments.

- Uses proper subject-verb agreement, pronoun agreement, and consistent verb tense.

- Uses correct capitalization, punctuation, and spelling.

Draft your final essay in the space below.

_____
_____
_____
_____
_____
_____
_____
_____
_____
_____
_____
_____
_____
_____
_____
_____
_____
_____
_____
_____
_____
_____

Name _____ Date _____

_____

_____

_____

_____

_____

_____

_____

_____

_____

_____

_____

_____

_____

_____

_____

_____

_____

_____

_____

_____

_____

_____

_____

_____

_____

_____

_____

_____

Writing Prompt 3: Narrative

Plan, write, and proofread a narrative in response to the writing prompt below.

Sometimes things happen to us that we don't expect. Write a story for a children's magazine about something surprising that happened to you. You can write the story about a real experience or an imaginary one. Describe what happened. Include characters and dialogue as you describe the events in the story.

As you write your essay, be sure to

- Focus on one topic.

- Include sensory details about the events in your story.

- Explain why the event was significant.

- Organize your writing and present your ideas in a logical order.

- Develop your characters so readers understand them.

- Edit your essay for correct grammar and usage.

Prewriting

1. **Analyze the Prompt.** Read the prompt carefully to identify the purpose of and the audience for your response.

Purpose

The prompt asks you to write a story about something surprising that happened to you. The story may be true or made up. The prompt tells you who your audience is and the format for your response.

Complete the following sentences:

The prompt asks me to write a _____.

The purpose of this kind of writing is to _____.

My audience is _____.

Audience

According to the prompt, who is your audience? Use the following step-by-step method to analyze the audience identified in the prompt.

Steps	Explanation	Your Response
Step 1 Ask yourself, "Who is the audience for this story?"	Look at the prompt. Who will most likely be reading your story?	
Step 2 Ask, "What will my audience expect when they read a children's magazine?"	Remember that your audience will want to know what the surprising thing was that happened.	
Step 3 Ask, "How can I keep my audience interested?"	Think about how to tell your story in a clear and interesting way. Do you want to make your story funny? scary? full of suspense?	

2. Brainstorm Story Ideas. Use the graphic organizer below to help you think about different topics you might write about. Choosing a story topic that interests you will greatly improve your writing and your ability to develop characters and events.

Surprising Event	What happened?	Why is it interesting?

3. **Develop Your Topic Idea.** Choose the surprising event that you want to write about. Then, choose the characters, setting, and events. The characters are the people or animals in the story. The setting is when and where the story takes place. The events are what happens in the story.

Use the graphic organizer to help you brainstorm parts of your story. Complete the boxes with the characters, setting, and events in the story.

Characters:

↓

Setting:
Where:

When:

↓

Surprising Event:

↓   ↓   ↓

Event 1:   **Event 2:**   **Event 3:**

Name _____ Date _____

4. **Organize Your Ideas.** Now that you have brainstormed the characters, setting, and events of your story, you will want to organize your ideas so that you can tell them in a logical order.

In the graphic organizer below, organize the events of your story into the beginning, middle, and end. The beginning part should introduce the event, the characters, and the setting. Remember to put story events in a logical order. Add details that you want to include in each box.

Beginning

Middle

End

Drafting Your Response

Use the following framework to draft your response to the narrative writing prompt. Write your draft on your own paper.

Framework	Directions and Explanations
Beginning	
Get your audience interested right away.	To get your audience interested, start with a statement or question that grabs readers' attention.
Explain the surprising experience and why it was important to you.	Tell your readers why the event was significant to you, such as what you learned.
Establish the setting and introduce the narrator or characters.	Help your readers understand where and when the story takes place and who it happens to.
Middle	
Describe the plot or main problem in the story.	Tell your readers what the main problem or surprising event is in the story. Explain the event in detail.
Develop characters.	Make your characters believable. Use dialogue and description to make characters come to life.
Present your ideas in a logical order.	Tell events in the order they occur. Use transition words to show how events are connected.
End	
Provide a conclusion to the events.	Explain how the story's problem is solved. Be sure the conclusion flows from the events in the story.

Evaluating, Revising, and Editing Your Response

Use the following strategies to evaluate and revise your response. You may make your revisions directly on your first draft, or, if necessary, write your revised draft on your own paper.

<table>
<tr><td colspan="3" align="center">Evaluation Guidelines for Narrative</td></tr>
<tr><th>Evaluation Questions</th><th>Tips</th><th>Revision Techniques</th></tr>
<tr>
<td>1. Does the story tell about an event that addresses the prompt?</td>
<td>Ask, "Does my response tell a story about a surprising event?"</td>
<td>If necessary, revise your purpose so that it addresses the prompt.</td>
</tr>
<tr>
<td>2. Is the response organized appropriately?</td>
<td>Check that events are presented in a logical order, such as the order they take place.</td>
<td>If necessary, change the order of events in your story.</td>
</tr>
<tr>
<td>3. Do you introduce the characters, setting, and events?</td>
<td>Ask, "Who are the characters in my story? What happens to them? When and where does it happen?"</td>
<td>Cut out unimportant characters or events. Add characters and events if needed to develop the story. Add details that tell when and where the story is happening.</td>
</tr>
<tr>
<td>4. Do you develop the characters and events?</td>
<td>Circle details that show what the characters are like. Underline details about the events.</td>
<td>Add descriptive details and dialogue if needed.</td>
</tr>
<tr>
<td>5. Does the story have a logical flow?</td>
<td>Look for transition words and phrases, such as first, next, then, and soon after.</td>
<td>Add linking words to show how events are connected.</td>
</tr>
<tr>
<td>6. Does the response use concrete words and phrases and sensory details?</td>
<td>Identify places where word choices can be stronger, more precise, and more descriptive.</td>
<td>Replace general words and phrases with precise words. Add sensory details.</td>
</tr>
<tr>
<td>7. Does the response include a strong conclusion?</td>
<td>Check for a concluding paragraph. Does it resolve the story's main problem?</td>
<td>Add a conclusion that logically ends the story.</td>
</tr>
</table>

Proofing Your Response

Final Proofreading Guidelines

Proofread your response to ensure that it

- Contains only complete sentences and no fragments.

- Uses proper subject-verb agreement, pronoun agreement, and consistent verb tense.

- Uses correct capitalization, punctuation, and spelling.

Draft your final essay in the space below.

_____

_____

_____

_____

_____

_____

_____

_____

_____

_____

_____

_____

_____

_____

_____

_____

_____

_____

_____

_____

_____

_____

Name _____ Date _____

Reading Practice Test

Literature

In this selection, a girl takes a class trip to a butterfly museum. Read the selection. Then, answer the questions. On your answer sheet, darken the circle for each correct answer for multiple-choice items. For the open-ended item, write your answer on a separate sheet of paper.

Carmen's Diary

May 17

Dear Diary,

I had a wonderful day! Our teacher took the entire class to the Concord Butterfly Museum. The whole museum is about butterflies. I thought I already knew all there was to know about butterflies. We studied them in science class with Mr. Neller. I was surprised at how much new information I learned on our field trip.

We met our museum guide as soon as we stepped off the bus. She handed each of us a worksheet called "The Great Museum Challenge." It had a list of clues that we had to follow to find the answers to questions. It was like a treasure hunt inside the museum.

Next, our class divided into pairs. Our guide gave us maps of the museum and told us that we could answer the questions in any order. She said that we could ask her or our teacher for help. She also said that we should try our best to answer all of the questions on our own. I was excited to begin, because I love playing detective and solving mysteries.

My partner was Raul. We decided to start with the first question, which asked, "What is the largest butterfly in the world?" The clue was a picture of a queen wearing a crown. Raul is good at understanding hints. He said that we should look for something with the word "queen" on it. I am good at using maps to find places. I looked at the museum map and saw that one room had a display called "Amazing Butterfly Facts." I led us there.

As soon as we walked into the room, Raul spotted a sign that said "Meet the Queen of Butterflies." We knew we had found the answer to the first question. The display showed a butterfly called Queen Alexandra's Birdwing. With its wings open, it was 11 inches wide! I was delighted that we had solved our first question.

After we wrote the answer, we chose our next question. It said, "A butterfly and a moth may look the same, but they are very different. What is one difference?" The clue was a picture of the sun. Raul and I discussed this clue. We both said what we thought it meant. Then, he said that we should try to find a display that compared butterflies and moths.

I looked at the map and saw a display called "Butterflies and Other Insects." The display was in an odd part of the museum. I followed the map closely, and soon Raul and I found what we were looking for. We later learned that some of our classmates spent much time trying to find their way through the museum to the display. When Raul and I reached the display, we saw that one of the glass cases had a sign on it that said "Moths." We read the information, and then the clue made sense! We learned that butterflies fly during the day, when the sun is out. Moths usually fly at night.

Raul and I were able to answer all of the questions on our worksheet by working together. When we finished, I cheered and gave him a high-five. Then, we went into the last room, which turned out to be our favorite. Displays of hundreds of beautiful butterflies filled the room. Tomorrow I will tell Carla all about the museum.

1. Read this sentence from the selection.

> "When we finished, I cheered
> and gave him a high-five."

Who is the speaker of this sentence?

A Raul

B Mr. Neller

C Carla

D Carmen

2. At the end of the selection, why are Carmen
    and Raul pleased?

A They will each get to take a butterfly
    home.

B They will be coming back to the
    museum the next day.

C They were able to answer all the
    questions on the worksheet.

D They were glad that it was time to go
    home.

3. Why was the last room Carmen and Raul's
    favorite?

A It was small.

B It was dark.

C It had hundreds of butterflies.

D It had the largest butterfly in the world.

4. What did Carmen and Raul learn at the
    museum?

A Butterflies fly during the day, while
    moths fly at night.

B Butterflies have colorful wings, while
    moths have dull wings.

C Butterflies are the largest insects in the
    world.

D Butterflies are attracted to bright lights.

5. What helps you understand that this selection is a diary entry?

   A It has a beginning, middle, and end.

   B It uses third-person point of view to tell about events.

   C It includes quotations of what people said.

   D It begins with a date and describes what a person did.

6. Why does the museum most likely give the children a worksheet when they arrive?

   A The museum wants visitors to have fun while they learn.

   B The museum wants visitors to have homework when they leave.

   C The museum needs help from visitors to find certain displays.

   D The museum wants visitors to pay attention when the guide speaks.

7. Why does Raul make a good partner for Carmen during the museum trip?

   A Raul is good at reading maps.

   B Raul is good at understanding clues.

   C Raul knows a lot about butterflies.

   D Raul has visited the museum before.

8. Which sentence **best** shows how Carmen feels about the museum?

   A I thought I already knew all there was to know about butterflies.

   B I was excited to begin, because I love playing detective and solving mysteries.

   C The display was in an odd part of the museum.

   D We later learned that some of our classmates spent much time trying to find their way through the museum to the display.

9. When Carmen tells Carla about the museum, what two things will she most likely tell her? Use information from the selection to support your response.

In this play, a family watches an important event in history. Read the play. Then, answer the questions. On your answer sheet, darken the circle for each correct answer for multiple-choice items. For the open-ended item, write your answer on a separate sheet of paper.

A Living Room Adventure

Cast List

Dad

Becky, 9 years old

Susan, 9 years old

Uncle Frank

Setting

A Houston family is watching television in their living room. Six hours earlier, the *Apollo 11* lunar module touched down on the moon.

DAD:	You'll remember this date for the rest of your life. 10:00 P.M. on July 20, 1969. The date that people first walked on the moon.

(BECKY and SUSAN, twin sisters, sit next to each other on the couch.)

BECKY:	We could have been watching this at Uncle Frank's house tonight, Susan. Except you never want to go anywhere so he had to come over here.
UNCLE FRANK:	*(To Becky)* It's no problem. I'm glad to be here. *(To Dad)* I can't believe this is really happening! They actually landed on the moon.
DAD:	Watch, kids. You're about to see history being made.
SUSAN:	*(Tossing back her hair)* So what if I like staying at home, Becky?

BECKY: You never want to do anything different. Or eat anything different. *(Imitating her sister's voice)* "I only eat peanut butter sandwiches for lunch and macaroni and cheese for dinner." I'm not like you. I like to have adventures. It's boring at home.

(BECKY jumps off the couch and sits on the floor, far away from her sister.)

DAD: I think if you stopped talking for a few minutes, Becky, you'd have an adventure right here in your own living room.

SUSAN: That's what you always say. Everything is boring.

UNCLE FRANK: I thought twins were supposed to be friends.

BECKY: We are friends. We're just different from each other.

SUSAN: And Becky is having trouble getting used to that.

BECKY: *(Sitting cross-legged on the floor with her elbows on her knees and her chin in her hands)* Susan should try something different once in a while.

DAD: Listen. One of the astronauts is talking. Neil Armstrong.

VOICE OF NEIL ARMSTRONG: I'm at the foot of the ladder. The lunar module footpads are only depressed in the surface about 1 or 2 inches. It's almost like a powder. I'm going to step off the ladder now.

BECKY: *(Lifting up her chin and pointing excitedly)* Look, he's stepping on the moon! What would that be like? Can you imagine?

SUSAN: I think it would be scary.

BECKY: He's really far from home! Can you imagine just stepping into some kind of strange powdery stuff that no human being has ever seen?

SUSAN: You're right. That would be kind of amazing.

BECKY: Dad, what happens if their spaceship breaks down? Will anyone be able to come help them?

DAD: I'm sure that we would think of some way to help them.

UNCLE FRANK: Look! He did it! He stepped off the ladder onto the moon!

VOICE OF ARMSTRONG: That's one small step for man, one giant leap for mankind.

SUSAN: *(Clapping her hands excitedly)* Think about this. He can look up and see Earth in the sky. Nobody has ever been able to do that before.

VOICE OF ARMSTRONG: It has a stark beauty all its own. It's like much of the high desert of the United States. It's different, but it's very pretty out here.

SUSAN: I do like the desert, Becky. Remember when we went to Arizona?

BECKY: *(Softly)* That would be terrible if they got stuck up there. With nobody around to help them.

(SUSAN gets off the couch and sits next to BECKY on the floor. She puts her arm around her sister.)

BECKY: *(Leaning against her)* I'm glad we're still home. It would have been weird to drive at night after seeing this. Wouldn't it? This moon landing is kind of scary.

SUSAN: I think it's kind of cool.

(BECKY and SUSAN look at each other. Then they burst out laughing.)

BECKY: What is wrong with this picture?

10. What does Neil Armstrong compare the moon to?

   A an ocean

   B a desert

   C Earth

   D a frozen lake

11. Read these lines from the play.

   > **BECKY:** *(Lifting up her chin and pointing excitedly)* Look, he's stepping on the moon! What would that be like? Can you imagine?

   The author uses the word *excitedly* to show the reader that Becky

   A is scared about what might happen.

   B wants Dad to turn up the sound on the TV.

   C sees something amazing happening.

   D is trying to get people's attention.

12. How would an actor use the words in parentheses in this play?

    A to figure out which lines to speak

    B to see who the characters are

    C to know what the setting is

    D to know how to move and speak

13. At the end of the play, what does Susan do to show that she forgives Becky?

    A She tosses back her hair.

    B She leans against her.

    C She sits beside her.

    D She imitates her voice.

14. How does Becky change during the play?

    A At first she is upset about not going out, but later she is glad the family stayed home to watch TV.

    B At first she is excited about watching the moon landing, but later she wishes she had done something else.

    C At first she is frightened about the astronauts, but later she realizes they are safe.

    D At first she wants to do the same things she always does, but later she decides to try new things.

15. Which statement **best** summarizes the play?

    A Neil Armstrong became the first human to walk on the moon on July 20, 1969.

    B While twin sisters watch the first moon landing on TV, they learn that they are more alike than different.

    C On a Saturday night in July 1969, a Houston family watches TV while twin sisters argue with each other.

    D Twin sisters watch the moon landing on TV and remember a time when they took a trip to Arizona.

16. What does Dad think about the television event the family is watching? Provide examples from the play that show how Dad feels.

Name _____ Date _____

In this poem, an unwelcome guest arrives in town. Read the poem. Then, answer the questions. On your answer sheet, darken the circle for each correct answer for multiple-choice items. For the open-ended item, write your answer on a separate sheet of paper.

An Unwelcome Guest

A wild, gray guest blows into town

And people pull their windows down.

Rushing up and down the streets,

She shoves at everyone she meets.

They race inside and slam their doors,

As this angry guest shrieks and roars.

"This storm," they cry, "is more than rain!

It is a serious hurricane!"

Denied our hospitality,

The wild guest tore through our city,

Ripped branches off the sides of trees

And forced the palm trees to their knees.

Her greenish clouds swirled until they burst.

Her manners were the very worst!

Rain poured down like water from a faucet.

Streets were streams, and if your car was there, you lost it.

After putting out every city light

And keeping us awake all night,

The storm blew out of town (she had no bags to pack).

But what a mess she left! We'll never ask her back.

17. Which words in the second stanza does the poet use to show that the guest is angry?

  A shrieks and roars

  B slam their doors

  C race inside

  D they cry

18. How does the speaker in the poem feel about the storm?

  A He is upset that it did so much damage.

  B He is thrilled by its power.

  C He is pleased that it brought a lot of rain.

  D He is afraid for the safety of his city.

19. Why did the poet most likely write this poem?

    A to explain how hurricanes form

    B to help the reader picture a serious storm

    C to tell a story about someone's adventure

    D to give information about different storms

20. What are the two main things that are being compared in this poem?

    A a homeowner and a houseguest

    B a hurricane and a rainstorm

    C an unwelcome guest and a hurricane

    D rain and wind

21. What is the theme of the poem?

    A Rainstorms can be severe, but hurricanes are often worse.

    B When you travel, unexpected things can happen.

    C During a bad storm, valuable things can be lost.

    D A hurricane is unwanted, and it can cause a lot of damage.

22. How do people who live in the city react to the "wild guest"?

    A They invite the guest inside.

    B They slam their doors on the guest.

    C They ask the guest to visit at another time.

    D They enjoy staying up all night with the guest.

23. In the third stanza, how does the poet compare trees to people?

    A The trees tear something.

    B The trees have branches ripped off them.

    C The trees have sides.

    D The trees are forced to their knees.

24. What language in the poem helps you understand that the guest is unwelcome? Give three examples from the poem.

Name _____ Date _____

Informational Text

In this selection, two men get help exploring land. On your answer sheet, darken the circle for each correct answer for multiple-choice items. For the open-ended item, write your answer on a separate sheet of paper.

The Lewis and Clark Expedition

In his first term as president, Thomas Jefferson nearly doubled the size of the United States in one move. He did this by buying a huge territory from the French government. This land came to be called the Louisiana Purchase. The land stretched west from the Mississippi River to the Rocky Mountains.

President Jefferson asked his secretary, Meriwether Lewis, to head an expedition to find out more about the new land. Lewis asked Lieutenant William Clark to lead it with him. Congress gave the expedition a budget of $2,500.

The plan was to travel up the Missouri River, then walk to the Columbia River, and finally travel by boat to the Pacific Ocean. Along the way, they would gather examples of plants and make notes about the animals. They would also make contact with the Native Americans who lived there.

The expedition started in May of 1804 with 33 members and 3 boats. In all, the group carried almost 4,000 pounds of supplies.

Reading Practice Test
Higher Scores on Reading and Language Arts, Grade 4

Some of the Supplies Taken on the Expedition

Camping Gear	150 yards of cloth for tents and sheets
	25 hatchets
	10.5 pounds of fishing hooks and lines
	12 pounds of soap
	193 pounds of soup paste made of meat and vegetables
	3 bushels of salt
Weapons	15 rifles
	24 large knives
	420 pounds of lead for bullets
	176 pounds of gunpowder
Gifts for Indian Tribes	144 pocket mirrors
	4,600 sewing needles
	144 small scissors
	10 pounds of sewing thread
	288 knives
	25 pounds of beads

Source: National Geographic

In the fall, the explorers arrived at a Mandan Indian village. There they hired a French trader to guide them through the unmapped region. The trader was accompanied by his Native American wife, Sacagawea. She proved to be a better guide and interpreter than her husband. She helped guide them through the unfamiliar territory.

After more than a year of exploring, the group reached the Continental Divide. This is the line at which the rivers start flowing west to the Pacific Ocean rather than east. They expected to find the Columbia River, but they could see only mountain after mountain stretching before them. Just when finding the river seemed hopeless, the explorers met a group of Shoshone Indians. Sacagawea recognized one of the chiefs as her own brother. He sold the group many horses and found them a guide. The horses allowed the expedition to get from the Missouri to the Columbia River.

More than two years after they began their journey, Lewis and Clark arrived back at their starting point in St. Louis, Missouri. The 1,000 residents of the city gathered along the shore to welcome the expedition home. People had believed that everyone had died on the expedition, so the news of their arrival was a cause for celebration.

The Lewis and Clark Expedition was one of the most important journeys ever taken in this country. Not only did Lewis and Clark help map the territory, but they also provided new information about the people, plants, and animals that lived there.

1. Why was the Shoshone guide probably able to help Lewis and Clark find their way through the mountains?

   A The guide was familiar with the region.

   B The guide spoke excellent English.

   C The guide was related to Sacagawea.

   D The guide had horses for carrying the group's gear.

2. Which of the following was within the Louisiana Purchase?

   A St. Louis

   B Washington, D.C.

   C the Columbia River

   D the Pacific Ocean

3. Why did the author most likely include details about Sacagawea in the selection?

   A to show the importance of Native Americans to the journey

   B to explain why the expedition brought gifts for Native Americans

   C to demonstrate the skills Native Americans had with horses

   D to show the conflicts the expedition had with Native Americans

4. What does the word territory mean in the first paragraph?

   A expedition

   B nation

   C government

   D region

5. What is the main way this selection is organized?

   A cause and effect

   B problem and solution

   C comparison and contrast

   D sequence

6. What is the main idea of this selection?

   A As president, Thomas Jefferson made the Louisiana Purchase and doubled the United States.

   B Lewis and Clark made a long and difficult journey to explore the Louisiana Purchase.

   C The United States bought the Louisiana Purchase from France.

   D Lewis and Clark packed a lot of supplies for their exploration of the Louisiana Purchase.

7. What can you tell about the supplies Lewis and Clark took based on the information in the chart?

   A They needed more weapons for hunting than the ones they brought.

   B The materials were bulky and heavy.

   C The Indians had no use for the gifts the expedition brought.

   D The materials were not very useful for the trip.

8. What evidence supports the idea that the expedition took longer than expected?

   A The expedition needed horses to get from the Missouri River to the Columbia River.

   B The expedition hired a French trader and his wife, Sacagawea, as guides and interpreters.

   C People celebrated when the expedition returned because they thought everyone had died.

   D There were no maps of the area, so Lewis and Clark made their own.

9. Why was Lewis and Clark's expedition important? Support your answer.

Name _____ Date _____

This selection describes how to make a tasty snack. Read the selection. Then, answer the questions. On your answer sheet, darken the circle for each correct answer for multiple-choice items. For the open-ended item, write your answer on a separate sheet of paper.

Pepitas: A Tasty Autumn Snack

Pepitas, or roasted pumpkin seeds, are easy to make and delicious to eat. This salty, crunchy treat is also a healthful snack. First, ask an adult to help you. Then, gather all the foods and tools in the list below. Ask the adult to find the kitchen knife.

What You Need

Ingredients	Tools
one pumpkin, any size	strainer
olive oil	large bowl
salt	measuring cups and spoons
	baking sheet
	oven
	kitchen knife

To begin preparing the pepitas, ask an adult to preheat the oven to 300° F. This will allow the oven time to heat up. Then, ask an adult to cut off the top of the pumpkin. The hole should be large enough so that you can fit your hand inside. Next, use your hands or a large spoon to scoop out all the seeds.

After you remove the seeds, you need to wash them. Place the seeds in a strainer, or a bowl with small holes in the bottom. Because the seeds are larger than the holes, the seeds will stay in the bowl, but the water will drain out. Rinse the seeds with cold water until they are clean.

Next, use a measuring cup to count how many cups of seeds you have. Then, measure 1 tablespoon of olive oil and 1/2 teaspoon of salt for every cup of seeds. For example, if you have 2 cups of seeds, then you need 2 tablespoons of olive oil and 1 teaspoon of salt. An adult can help you measure.

Next, mix the oil and seeds together in a large bowl. Make sure that all the seeds are coated with oil. Then, spread the seeds in one layer on the baking sheet. Finally, lightly <u>sprinkle</u> salt over the seeds. Now you are ready to cook the seeds!

Have an adult place the baking sheet in the oven. The seeds should cook for about 45 minutes. An adult needs to stir the seeds every 5 minutes so that they do not burn. You will know when the seeds are done because they will be brown and crispy.

After the seeds have finished cooking, have an adult remove them from the oven. Allow the seeds to cool, and then enjoy a delicious snack!

This diagram shows the nine steps you can follow to make pepitas.

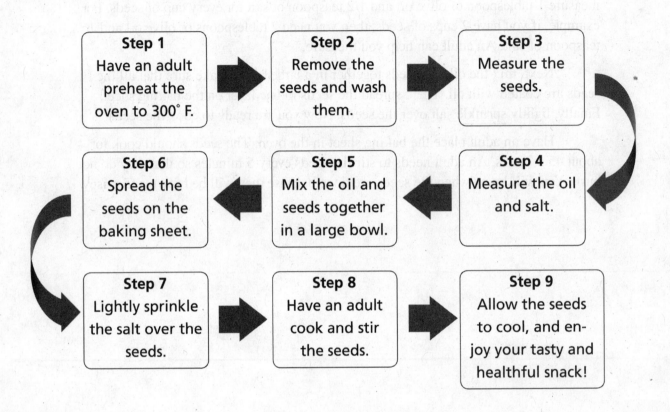

Step 1
Have an adult preheat the oven to 300° F.

Step 2
Remove the seeds and wash them.

Step 3
Measure the seeds.

Step 6
Spread the seeds on the baking sheet.

Step 5
Mix the oil and seeds together in a large bowl.

Step 4
Measure the oil and salt.

Step 7
Lightly sprinkle the salt over the seeds.

Step 8
Have an adult cook and stir the seeds.

Step 9
Allow the seeds to cool, and enjoy your tasty and healthful snack!

10. Based on the diagram, what tool do you need to complete Step 2?

   A measuring cups

   B strainer

   C baking sheet

   D oven

11. Which sentence from the selection contains the author's opinion?

   A Next, mix the oil and seeds together in a large bowl.

   B The seeds should cook for about 45 minutes.

   C Pepitas, or roasted pumpkin seeds, are easy to make and delicious to eat.

   D An adult needs to stir the seeds every 5 minutes so that they do not burn.

12. According to the selection, why do the seeds need to be stirred while they are baking?

    A to keep them from burning

    B to coat them evenly with oil

    C to give them a salty taste

    D to make them turn brown

13. Why do you need to measure how many cups of seeds you have?

    A to find the cooking temperature for the seeds

    B to know how long you need to cook the seeds

    C to decide what size baking sheet you will need

    D to figure out how much oil and salt you will need

14. Which of these would be a good title for the selection?

    A What Are Pepitas?

    B Things to Do with Pumpkins

    C How to Make Pepitas

    D Healthful Snack Ideas

15. What does the word sprinkle mean in this selection?

    A divide

    B heat

    C cook

    D shake

16. Explain why children should get help from an adult when making pepitas.

Language Arts and Vocabulary
Practice Test

Language Arts Practice Test

Choose the correct word to complete each sentence. On your answer sheet, darken the circle for each correct answer for multiple-choice items. For the short-answer item, write your answer on a separate sheet of paper.

Yellowstone National Park has some of the most unusual scenery in the country. Great Fountain Geyser sometimes (1) water higher than a twenty-story building. Yellowstone Lake is our country's (2) high-altitude lake. (3) sparkling water seems shinier than a mirror. The smell of pine trees (4) the air. Yellowstone has a deep canyon. But the Grand Canyon in Arizona is deeper. In addition, the park has about 10,000 hot springs with steam rising up to the sky. You (5) visit this amazing place if you ever have the chance.

1. What word should fill in blank 1?

   A has

   B shoots

   C drips

   D leaks

2. Using the correct form of the adjective "large," rewrite the second sentence (sentence with blank 2).

3. What word should fill in blank 3?

   A Your

   B Our

   C Their

   D Its

4. What word should fill in blank 4?

   A fills

   B fill

   C filled

   D filling

5. What word should fill in blank 5?

   A shall

   B should

   C will

   D might

Choose the correct word or words to complete each sentence. On your answer sheet, darken the circle for each correct answer for multiple-choice items. For the short-answer item, write your answer on a separate sheet of paper.

Do you get enough sleep? Most fourth-grade students need about eight or nine hours of sleep each night. Children (6) get enough sleep are better able to learn in school. If you don't get enough sleep, (7) things could happen to you. You (8) get angry more easily. You could have more accidents. You might even forget (9) you are. Nighttime sleep is important, but so are naps. Naps (10) a good way to get some extra rest.

6. What word should fill in blank 6?

  A which

  B when

  C what

  D who

7. What word should fill in blank 7?

  A strangest

  B stranger

  C strangely

  D strange

8. What word or words should fill in blank 8?

  A might

  B ought to

  C would

  D must

9. What word should fill in blank 9?

  A wear

  B where

  C were

  D we're

10. Using the correct form of the verb "to be," rewrite the last sentence (sentence with blank 10).

For numbers 11–15, choose the word or words that best complete each sentence. On your answer sheet, darken the circle for each correct answer.

11. Petra bought a _____ purse last week.

    A red leather huge

    B huge red leather

    C leather red huge

    D leather huge red

12. My sister and _____ are going to the park because we love to play there.

    A me

    B I

    C we

    D us

13. Near the end of the race, Todd _____ ahead and edged out the other runners for a victory.

    A sprinted

    B went

    C got

    D wandered

14. Our family _____ to the beach next month.

    A will be going

    B going

    C has been going

    D gone

15. Mr. Wagner's class is going _____ the museum.

    A two

    B too

    C though

    D to

Read each question and choose the best answer. On your answer sheet, darken the circle for each correct answer.

16. Choose the sentence that is written correctly.

    A Cara has more money saved than he has.

    B Cara has more money saved then he has.

    C Cara has most money saved than he has.

    D Cara has more money saved than him has.

17. Choose the sentence that is written correctly.

    A The cat up into the tree chased the squirrel.

    B Up, into the tree, the cat chased the squirrel.

    C The cat chased the squirrel up into the tree.

    D The cat chased up into the tree the squirrel.

18. Find the sentence that **best** combines the following sentences.

    Rick chased after the dog.
    He was too slow to catch it.

    A Rick chased after the dog, so he was too slow to catch it.

    B Although he was too slow, Rick chased after the dog.

    C The dog was too slow, although Rick chased after it.

    D Rick chased after the dog, but he was too slow to catch it.

19. Find the sentence that is complete and is written correctly.

    A To plan the party, met on Tuesday.

    B The most beautiful statue in the whole museum.

    C When Grace wore her lovely new sweater.

    D The market on Main Street has tasty peaches.

20. Read these sentences. What is the **best** way to rewrite them for a formal paper?

    Hummingbirds are really cool.
    You can't even see their wings
    move because they go fast, like
    up to 200 beats a second.

    A Hummingbirds are really cool. You can't even see their wings move. That's because they go fast, like up to 200 beats a second.

    B A hummingbird's wings can beat up to 200 times a second. At these speeds, it is difficult to see their wings move.

    C Hummingbirds, which are really cool, move their wings really fast. It can even be 200 beats a second.

    D You can't even see a hummingbird's wings move because they go super fast, like up to 200 beats a second.

Identify the type of error, if any, in each underlined section. On your answer sheet, darken the circle for each correct answer.

<u>Some authers don't use</u> their real name when they write books. <u>Instead, they</u>
21   22

<u>use a pen name.</u> When he was a <u>young man, Samuel clemens used</u> to guide
                                                                 23

boats on the Mississippi River. He always liked sailing on the Mississippi

<u>River When the water was</u> two fathoms deep, a guide always called
24

out "mark twain." Clemens <u>liked the way those words sounded.</u> He signed all
                                                    25

his books, including *Tom Sawyer*, with his pen name, Mark Twain.

21. What is the error in underlined section 21?

   A Spelling

   B Capitalization

   C Punctuation

   D No Error

22. What is the error in underlined section 22?

   A Spelling

   B Capitalization

   C Punctuation

   D No Error

23. What is the error in underlined section 23?

   A Spelling

   B Capitalization

   C Punctuation

   D No Error

24. What is the error in underlined section 24?

   A Spelling

   B Capitalization

   C Punctuation

   D No Error

25. What is the error in underlined section 25?

   A Spelling

   B Capitalization

   C Punctuation

   D No Error

Identify the type of error, if any, in each underlined section. On your answer sheet, darken the circle for each correct answer for the multiple-choice items. For the short-answer item, write your answer on a separate sheet of paper.

Mountain gorillas live in the mountain <u>forests of africa, usually in</u>
26

<u>groups of about ten! At night</u> the gorillas sleep in trees or on the
27

ground, and during the day they look for food. <u>They most often eat</u>
28

<u>roots and tree bark but they find other plants to eat, too.</u> Mountain

gorillas are shy animals, and they are almost always gentle. A group

of gorillas <u>may axcept a scientist.</u> Then the scientist might live
29

among them <u>for a while to studdy them.</u>
30

---

26. What is the error in underlined section 26?

  A Spelling

  B Capitalization

  C Punctuation

  D No Error

27. What is the error in underlined section 27?

  A Spelling

  B Capitalization

  C Punctuation

  D No Error

28. Rewrite the third sentence correctly (underlined section 28).

29. What is the error in underlined section 29?

  A Spelling

  B Capitalization

  C Punctuation

  D No Error

30. What is the error in underlined section 30?

  A Spelling

  B Capitalization

  C Punctuation

  D No Error

Read each question and choose the best answer. On your answer sheet, darken the circle for each correct answer.

31. Choose the sentence that shows the **correct** punctuation.

   A "Jane," "did you see that flash of light?" asked Nicki.

   B "Jane, did you see that flash of light?" asked Nicki.

   C "Jane, did you see that flash of light? asked Nicki."

   D "Jane," did you see that flash of light?" asked Nicki.

32. Choose the answer that shows the **correct** punctuation.

   A "What's your name? asked Bob."

   B "What's your name? asked Bob.

   C What's your name? "asked Bob."

   D "What's your name?" asked Bob.

33. Choose the sentence that is correct.

   A My aunt was born on April 25 1976, in Cleveland, Ohio.

   B My aunt was born on April 25, 1976, in Cleveland, Ohio.

   C My aunt was born on April 25, 1976, in Cleveland Ohio.

   D My aunt was born on April, 25, 1976 in Cleveland, Ohio.

34. Choose the correct word to complete the sentence.

> Our dog _____ 33 pounds last year.

   A wade

   B wayed

   C waighed

   D weighed

Read each question and choose the best answer. On your answer sheet, darken the circle for each correct answer.

35. Choose the answer that shows the **correct** punctuation.

   A Randall! come inside now! There's a tornado warning!

   B Randall. Come inside now. There's a tornado warning.

   C Randall come inside now? There's a tornado warning!

   D Randall, come inside now! There's a tornado warning.

36. Choose the answer that shows the **correct** punctuation.

   A We hiked, in the woods, rode our bikes, on trails, and swam in the lake.

   B We hiked in the woods rode our bikes on trails and swam in the lake.

   C We hiked in the woods, rode our bikes on trails, and swam in the lake.

   D We hiked, in the woods, rode our bikes, on trails, and swam, in the lake.

37. Choose the sentence that is correct.

   A When we visited Arches National Park in Utah, we saw rock arches.

   B When we visited Arches National Park in Utah we saw rock arches.

   C When we visited "Arches National Park" in Utah, we saw rock arches.

   D When we visited arches national park in Utah, we saw rock arches.

38. Choose the correct word to complete the sentence.

> Finishing the hike took a lot of _____.

   A effert

   B effit

   C efort

   D effort

Vocabulary Practice Test

Read the selection below. Then, answer the questions. On your answer sheet, darken the circle for each correct answer.

Siberian tigers live mostly in forests of eastern Russia and are the world's largest cats. The Siberian tiger spends much of its time hunting. First, it searches for <u>prey</u> such as wild boar or deer. It <u>creeps</u> to within 30 to 80 feet of the animal. Then, the tiger pounces and grabs the prey by the back of the neck, killing it. The tiger drags the animal into cover, where it <u>eats its fill</u>. It covers the remains to eat later, after it has rested.

1. What does the word <u>prey</u> mean in this selection?

   A an animal that hunts

   B an animal hunted for food

   C a place to live in

   D an area covered with trees

2. What does the word <u>creeps</u> help you understand about Siberian tigers?

   A They get very close to animals.

   B They make a lot of noise as they move.

   C They walk normally through the forest.

   D They sneak up on animals.

3. What does the phrase <u>eats its fill</u> mean in this selection?

   A The tiger digs a hole and then fills it in with dirt.

   B The tiger moves the animal out of sight.

   C The tiger has as much food as it wants.

   D The tiger eats the remains of an animal it caught earlier.

Read the selection below. Then, answer the questions. On your answer sheet, darken the circle for each correct answer.

Wee Willie Keeler of Baltimore set a major league baseball record in 1897—getting a hit in 44 straight games. During the summer of 1941, New York Yankee Joe DiMaggio surpassed 44 games and broke Keeler's record.

Newspapers reported on Joe's hitting streak every day. How long could his streak last? When would it end? Joe was modest and humble about his talent. He was never boastful.

By the night of July 17, 1941, Joe had made a hit in 55 straight games. During his 56th game, he was tagged out his first two times at bat. Then, in the eighth inning, Joe hit the ball. However, he was out in a double play. Joe's historic streak was over.

Joe's teammates thought he'd be upset, but he wasn't. Joe walked into the locker room and said, "Well, that's over."

The newspapers called him "Joltin' Joe DiMaggio." A popular song was written about his hitting streak. Yet through it all, Joe remained modest and unassuming.

4. What does surpassed mean in this selection?

   A played well

   B went beyond

   C set a record

   D passed over

5. Which word in the selection is an antonym, or opposite, of modest?

   A humble

   B talent

   C boastful

   D upset

6. What does the word historic mean in this selection?

   A making history

   B very old

   C without history

   D a person in history

Answer the questions. On your answer sheet, darken the circle for each correct answer.

7. Choose the word that **best** completes the blank.

> Broom is to sweep as shovel
> is to _____.

  A mess

  B dig

  C hole

  D hoe

8. Read these sentences. Choose the word that **best** completes **both** sentences.

> Throw the _____ in the basket.
> I _____ to go into town with you.

  A refuse

  B trash

  C paper

  D want

9. Read the sentence.

> The full moon hung in the
> sky like a pale balloon.

Why does the author compare the moon to a balloon?

  A to show that the moon is full of air

  B to show that the moon is light

  C to show that the moon is bright

  D to show that the moon is round

Name _____ Date _____

Answer the questions. On your answer sheet, darken the circle for each correct answer.

10. Read these sentences. Which word **best** completes **both** sentences?

> They will _____ the speech.
> The athlete broke the school _____.

A enjoy

B hear

C record

D trophy

11. Read these sentences. Which word is a clue about the meaning of the word <u>habitat</u>?

> The <u>habitat</u> of prairie dogs is open grassland on the prairies. There, they dig complicated underground homes for sleeping and raising their young.

A open

B dig

C homes

D young

12. Which word **best** completes this sentence?

> Heather is a very _____ person. She draws, paints, and even writes poetry.

A creative

B creation

C recreate

D creator

Writing Practice Test

Writing Prompt 1: Opinion

Plan, write, and proofread an opinion letter in response to the writing prompt below.

Some school districts are changing their school calendar so that students attend school year round, without a long summer break. Some people believe year-round school helps children learn better because they don't have a long break from learning.

Write an opinion letter to your local newspaper. Tell them what you think about year-round schools. Support your opinion with reasons.

As you write your letter, be sure to

- Focus on the topic.

- Explain your opinion.

- Give reasons for your opinion and support the reasons with details and examples.

- Organize your opinion letter so that your ideas have a logical order.

- Keep your audience in mind as you write.

- Edit your letter for correct grammar and usage.

Writing Prompt 2: Informative

Plan, write, and proofread an informative essay in response to the writing prompt below.

> Write an essay for your community newsletter about your favorite season of the year. Explain what that season is like and why it is your favorite. Include examples to support your ideas.

As you write your essay, be sure to

- Focus on one season.
- Clearly state your main idea.
- Describe the season in detail.
- Organize your writing and present your ideas in a logical order.
- Keep your audience in mind as you write.
- Edit your essay for correct grammar and usage.

Writing Prompt 3: Narrative

Plan, write, and proofread a narrative story in response to the writing prompt below.

Write a story for a children's magazine about the best day you ever had. You can write the story about a real experience or an imaginary one. Describe in detail what happened to make it the best day. Include characters, setting, and dialogue as you describe the events in the story.

As you write your essay, be sure to

- Focus on one topic.

- Include sensory details about the events in your story.

- Explain why the day was significant.

- Organize your writing and present your ideas in a logical order.

- Develop your characters so readers understand them.

- Edit your essay for correct grammar and usage.

Answer Sheets and Answer Key

Answer Sheets

Reading Practice: Literature

1 Ⓐ Ⓑ Ⓒ Ⓓ
2 Ⓐ Ⓑ Ⓒ Ⓓ
3 Ⓐ Ⓑ Ⓒ Ⓓ
4 Ⓐ Ⓑ Ⓒ Ⓓ
5 Ⓐ Ⓑ Ⓒ Ⓓ
6 Ⓐ Ⓑ Ⓒ Ⓓ
7 Write answers on a separate
sheet of paper.
8 Ⓐ Ⓑ Ⓒ Ⓓ
9 Ⓐ Ⓑ Ⓒ Ⓓ
10 Ⓐ Ⓑ Ⓒ Ⓓ
11 Ⓐ Ⓑ Ⓒ Ⓓ

12 Write answers on a separate
sheet of paper.
13 Ⓐ Ⓑ Ⓒ Ⓓ
14 Ⓐ Ⓑ Ⓒ Ⓓ
15 Ⓐ Ⓑ Ⓒ Ⓓ
16 Ⓐ Ⓑ Ⓒ Ⓓ
17 Ⓐ Ⓑ Ⓒ Ⓓ
18 Write answers on a separate
sheet of paper.
19 Ⓐ Ⓑ Ⓒ Ⓓ
20 Ⓐ Ⓑ Ⓒ Ⓓ
21 Ⓐ Ⓑ Ⓒ Ⓓ

22 Ⓐ Ⓑ Ⓒ Ⓓ
23 Write answers on a separate
sheet of paper.
24 Ⓐ Ⓑ Ⓒ Ⓓ
25 Ⓐ Ⓑ Ⓒ Ⓓ
26 Ⓐ Ⓑ Ⓒ Ⓓ
27 Ⓐ Ⓑ Ⓒ Ⓓ
28 Ⓐ Ⓑ Ⓒ Ⓓ
29 Write answers on a separate
sheet of paper.

Reading Practice: Informational Text

1 Ⓐ Ⓑ Ⓒ Ⓓ
2 Ⓐ Ⓑ Ⓒ Ⓓ
3 Ⓐ Ⓑ Ⓒ Ⓓ
4 Ⓐ Ⓑ Ⓒ Ⓓ
5 Ⓐ Ⓑ Ⓒ Ⓓ
6 Ⓐ Ⓑ Ⓒ Ⓓ
7 Write answers on a separate
sheet of paper.
8 Ⓐ Ⓑ Ⓒ Ⓓ
9 Ⓐ Ⓑ Ⓒ Ⓓ

10 Ⓐ Ⓑ Ⓒ Ⓓ
11 Ⓐ Ⓑ Ⓒ Ⓓ
12 Ⓐ Ⓑ Ⓒ Ⓓ
13 Ⓐ Ⓑ Ⓒ Ⓓ
14 Write answers on a separate
sheet of paper.
15 Ⓐ Ⓑ Ⓒ Ⓓ
16 Ⓐ Ⓑ Ⓒ Ⓓ
17 Ⓐ Ⓑ Ⓒ Ⓓ
18 Ⓐ Ⓑ Ⓒ Ⓓ

19 Ⓐ Ⓑ Ⓒ Ⓓ
20 Write answers on a separate
sheet of paper.
21 Ⓐ Ⓑ Ⓒ Ⓓ
22 Ⓐ Ⓑ Ⓒ Ⓓ
23 Ⓐ Ⓑ Ⓒ Ⓓ
24 Ⓐ Ⓑ Ⓒ Ⓓ
25 Ⓐ Ⓑ Ⓒ Ⓓ
26 Write answers on a separate
sheet of paper.

Language Arts Practice

1 (A) (B) (C) (D)
2 Write answers on a separate sheet of paper.
3 (A) (B) (C) (D)
4 (A) (B) (C) (D)
5 (A) (B) (C) (D)
6 Write answers on a separate sheet of paper.
7 (A) (B) (C) (D)
8 (A) (B) (C) (D)
9 (A) (B) (C) (D)
10 (A) (B) (C) (D)
11 (A) (B) (C) (D)
12 (A) (B) (C) (D)
13 (A) (B) (C) (D)

14 (A) (B) (C) (D)
15 (A) (B) (C) (D)
16 (A) (B) (C) (D)
17 (A) (B) (C) (D)
18 (A) (B) (C) (D)
19 (A) (B) (C) (D)
20 (A) (B) (C) (D)
21 (A) (B) (C) (D)
22 (A) (B) (C) (D)
23 Write answers on a separate sheet of paper.
24 (A) (B) (C) (D)
25 (A) (B) (C) (D)
26 (A) (B) (C) (D)
27 (A) (B) (C) (D)

28 (A) (B) (C) (D)
29 (A) (B) (C) (D)
30 Write answers on a separate sheet of paper.
31 (A) (B) (C) (D)
32 (A) (B) (C) (D)
33 (A) (B) (C) (D)
34 (A) (B) (C) (D)
35 (A) (B) (C) (D)
36 (A) (B) (C) (D)
37 (A) (B) (C) (D)
38 (A) (B) (C) (D)
39 (A) (B) (C) (D)
40 (A) (B) (C) (D)

Vocabulary Practice

1 (A) (B) (C) (D)
2 (A) (B) (C) (D)
3 (A) (B) (C) (D)
4 (A) (B) (C) (D)
5 (A) (B) (C) (D)

6 (A) (B) (C) (D)
7 (A) (B) (C) (D)
8 (A) (B) (C) (D)
9 (A) (B) (C) (D)
10 (A) (B) (C) (D)

11 (A) (B) (C) (D)
12 (A) (B) (C) (D)
13 (A) (B) (C) (D)
14 (A) (B) (C) (D)
15 (A) (B) (C) (D)

Writing Practice

Write your final responses to the writing prompts in the space provided.

Reading Practice Test: Literature

1 Ⓐ Ⓑ Ⓒ Ⓓ
2 Ⓐ Ⓑ Ⓒ Ⓓ
3 Ⓐ Ⓑ Ⓒ Ⓓ
4 Ⓐ Ⓑ Ⓒ Ⓓ
5 Ⓐ Ⓑ Ⓒ Ⓓ
6 Ⓐ Ⓑ Ⓒ Ⓓ
7 Ⓐ Ⓑ Ⓒ Ⓓ
8 Ⓐ Ⓑ Ⓒ Ⓓ
9 Write answers on a separate sheet of paper.

10 Ⓐ Ⓑ Ⓒ Ⓓ
11 Ⓐ Ⓑ Ⓒ Ⓓ
12 Ⓐ Ⓑ Ⓒ Ⓓ
13 Ⓐ Ⓑ Ⓒ Ⓓ
14 Ⓐ Ⓑ Ⓒ Ⓓ
15 Ⓐ Ⓑ Ⓒ Ⓓ
16 Write answers on a separate sheet of paper.
17 Ⓐ Ⓑ Ⓒ Ⓓ
18 Ⓐ Ⓑ Ⓒ Ⓓ

19 Ⓐ Ⓑ Ⓒ Ⓓ
20 Ⓐ Ⓑ Ⓒ Ⓓ
21 Ⓐ Ⓑ Ⓒ Ⓓ
22 Ⓐ Ⓑ Ⓒ Ⓓ
23 Ⓐ Ⓑ Ⓒ Ⓓ
24 Write answers on a separate sheet of paper.

Reading Practice Test: Informational Text

1 Ⓐ Ⓑ Ⓒ Ⓓ
2 Ⓐ Ⓑ Ⓒ Ⓓ
3 Ⓐ Ⓑ Ⓒ Ⓓ
4 Ⓐ Ⓑ Ⓒ Ⓓ
5 Ⓐ Ⓑ Ⓒ Ⓓ
6 Ⓐ Ⓑ Ⓒ Ⓓ

7 Ⓐ Ⓑ Ⓒ Ⓓ
8 Ⓐ Ⓑ Ⓒ Ⓓ
9 Write answers on a separate sheet of paper.
10 Ⓐ Ⓑ Ⓒ Ⓓ
11 Ⓐ Ⓑ Ⓒ Ⓓ
12 Ⓐ Ⓑ Ⓒ Ⓓ

13 Ⓐ Ⓑ Ⓒ Ⓓ
14 Ⓐ Ⓑ Ⓒ Ⓓ
15 Ⓐ Ⓑ Ⓒ Ⓓ
16 Write answers on a separate sheet of paper.

Language Arts Practice Test

1 Ⓐ Ⓑ Ⓒ Ⓓ

2 Write answers on a separate sheet of paper.

3 Ⓐ Ⓑ Ⓒ Ⓓ

4 Ⓐ Ⓑ Ⓒ Ⓓ

5 Ⓐ Ⓑ Ⓒ Ⓓ

6 Ⓐ Ⓑ Ⓒ Ⓓ

7 Ⓐ Ⓑ Ⓒ Ⓓ

8 Ⓐ Ⓑ Ⓒ Ⓓ

9 Ⓐ Ⓑ Ⓒ Ⓓ

10 Write answers on a separate sheet of paper.

11 Ⓐ Ⓑ Ⓒ Ⓓ

12 Ⓐ Ⓑ Ⓒ Ⓓ

13 Ⓐ Ⓑ Ⓒ Ⓓ

14 Ⓐ Ⓑ Ⓒ Ⓓ

15 Ⓐ Ⓑ Ⓒ Ⓓ

16 Ⓐ Ⓑ Ⓒ Ⓓ

17 Ⓐ Ⓑ Ⓒ Ⓓ

18 Ⓐ Ⓑ Ⓒ Ⓓ

19 Ⓐ Ⓑ Ⓒ Ⓓ

20 Ⓐ Ⓑ Ⓒ Ⓓ

21 Ⓐ Ⓑ Ⓒ Ⓓ

22 Ⓐ Ⓑ Ⓒ Ⓓ

23 Ⓐ Ⓑ Ⓒ Ⓓ

24 Ⓐ Ⓑ Ⓒ Ⓓ

25 Ⓐ Ⓑ Ⓒ Ⓓ

26 Ⓐ Ⓑ Ⓒ Ⓓ

27 Ⓐ Ⓑ Ⓒ Ⓓ

28 Write answers on a separate sheet of paper.

29 Ⓐ Ⓑ Ⓒ Ⓓ

30 Ⓐ Ⓑ Ⓒ Ⓓ

31 Ⓐ Ⓑ Ⓒ Ⓓ

32 Ⓐ Ⓑ Ⓒ Ⓓ

33 Ⓐ Ⓑ Ⓒ Ⓓ

34 Ⓐ Ⓑ Ⓒ Ⓓ

35 Ⓐ Ⓑ Ⓒ Ⓓ

36 Ⓐ Ⓑ Ⓒ Ⓓ

37 Ⓐ Ⓑ Ⓒ Ⓓ

38 Ⓐ Ⓑ Ⓒ Ⓓ

Vocabulary Practice Test

1 Ⓐ Ⓑ Ⓒ Ⓓ

2 Ⓐ Ⓑ Ⓒ Ⓓ

3 Ⓐ Ⓑ Ⓒ Ⓓ

4 Ⓐ Ⓑ Ⓒ Ⓓ

5 Ⓐ Ⓑ Ⓒ Ⓓ

6 Ⓐ Ⓑ Ⓒ Ⓓ

7 Ⓐ Ⓑ Ⓒ Ⓓ

8 Ⓐ Ⓑ Ⓒ Ⓓ

9 Ⓐ Ⓑ Ⓒ Ⓓ

10 Ⓐ Ⓑ Ⓒ Ⓓ

11 Ⓐ Ⓑ Ⓒ Ⓓ

12 Ⓐ Ⓑ Ⓒ Ⓓ

Writing Practice Test

Write your final responses to the writing prompts on your own paper.

Answer Key

Reading Practice: Literature

1. C
2. A
3. C
4. D
5. B
6. B
7. Possible response: Anna's day was special because she got to see the sea creatures that she was very interested in, including a seal show. She also got to see the dolphins and got a dolphin pin from the trainer.
8. C
9. D
10. B
11. D
12. Possible response: The journey was difficult because there was wildlife like skunks along the way. People's possessions had to be carried by horse. The trail was rocky, and it had large boulders on it.
13. D
14. B
15. B
16. C
17. A
18. Possible response: At the beginning of the play, Lucy wants to watch TV instead of trying something new. After she plants the flowers, she learns that she enjoys gardening and looks forward to doing more of it in the spring.
19. A
20. B
21. C
22. C
23. Possible response: The poet uses images to help readers imagine the prairie. For example, she writes that the prairie is like a sea of grass and it ripples like ocean waves. She also describes how the prairie sounds in the wind and how she feels like a part of it when the wind blows.
24. D
25. B
26. C
27. A
28. A
29. Possible response: The speaker really enjoys his trip. At the beginning, he mentions that his excitement grew before the trip. Then, he describes how animals seem like they are having fun, and he uses humor to describe the snakes. In the last stanza, he explains how much fun he had and how much he loved seeing the animals.

Reading Practice: Informational Text

1. D
2. A
3. C
4. D
5. B
6. B
7. Possible response: As a gas in the air, water condenses and forms clouds. When the clouds are full, they release the water as precipitation that falls to Earth. When the sun heats the water that has fallen to Earth, the water evaporates, returning to the air. Then, the cycle begins again.
8. A
9. B
10. D
11. D

12. B

13. C

14. Possible response: In colonial America, men did more of the hard physical work. For example, men cut trees and built homes and furniture. Women worked mostly inside the home, making yarn, clothing, soap, and candles. Women also did the cooking.

15. D

16. B

17. C

18. C

19. A

20. Possible response: The author wrote this selection to explain how to do something. The selection lists the ingredients you will need. It also tells you what to do and when to do it.

21. D

22. B

23. C

24. C

25. A

26. Possible response: Children probably enjoy making play dough because they like to mix things with their hands. It's also fun and easy to make play dough. After they make the play dough, children get to play with it.

Language Arts Practice

1. B

2. Geckos can shed their tails when they are attacked by another animal.

3. A

4. C

5. C

6. Have you ever heard a dog sing?

7. C

8. D

9. A

10. D

11. A

12. B

13. C

14. D

15. C

16. A

17. B

18. D

19. C

20. B

21. C

22. A

23. December, January, and February had been especially dry.

24. C

25. C

26. C

27. B

28. A

29. C

30. Linda's new puppy liked her, too.

31. B

32. A

33. B

34. D

35. A

36. B

37. C

38. D

39. A

40. C

Vocabulary Practice

1. B
2. A
3. D
4. B
5. C
6. C
7. D
8. D
9. A
10. C
11. C
12. C
13. C
14. B
15. B

Writing Practice

See Scoring Rubrics on pages 55–57.

Prompt 1: Students should write a letter describing a rule and giving their opinion about how the rule should be changed. Students should give reasons to support their opinion.

Prompt 2: Students should write an essay in which they describe a celebration or holiday and give details that explain why the holiday is important to them or their family.

Prompt 3: Students should write a true or made-up story for children about something surprising that happened to them. They should include characters and dialogue, as well as sensory details.

Reading Practice Test: Literature

1. D
2. C
3. C
4. A
5. D
6. A
7. B
8. B
9. Possible response: Carmen will most likely describe how the trip to the museum was like a treasure hunt. She will probably also tell Carla about her favorite part of the museum, which was the room filled with hundreds of butterflies.
10. B
11. C
12. D
13. C
14. A
15. B
16. Possible response: Dad thinks the moon landing is an important event. At the beginning, Dad tells the twins that they will always remember this event. He mentions that it is "history being made." He tells the girls to listen and pay attention when Neil Armstrong speaks.
17. A
18. A
19. B
20. C
21. D
22. B
23. D
24. Possible response: To show that the storm is unwelcome, the poet describes how people try to keep it out. For example, they pull down their windows and slam their doors. The poet also describes rude things the storm does. It shoves at people, it's angry, and it shrieks and roars. Finally, the guest causes a lot of damage, such as ripping branches from trees, bending palm trees, and knocking out lights.

Reading Practice Test: Informational Text

1. A
2. C
3. A
4. D
5. D
6. B
7. B
8. C
9. Possible response: The expedition was important because Lewis and Clark were exploring a huge new area of land that the United States had purchased. They made maps of the area, they made contact with Native Americans, and they studied the plants and animals found there.
10. B
11. C
12. A
13. D
14. C
15. D
16. Possible response: To make pepitas, you must do things that can be dangerous, like cut with a knife and use a hot oven. For safety, an adult should do these things.

Language Arts Practice Test

1. B
2. Yellowstone Lake is our country's largest high-altitude lake.
3. D
4. A
5. B
6. D
7. D
8. A
9. B
10. Naps are a good way to get some extra rest.
11. B
12. B
13. A

14. A
15. D
16. A
17. C
18. D
19. D
20. B
21. A
22. D
23. B
24. C
25. D
26. B
27. C
28. They most often eat roots and tree bark, but they find other plants to eat, too.
29. A
30. A
31. B
32. D
33. B
34. D
35. D
36. C
37. A
38. D

Vocabulary Practice Test

1. B
2. D
3. C
4. B
5. C
6. A
7. B
8. A
9. D
10. C
11. C
12. A

Writing Practice Test

See Scoring Rubrics on pages 55–57.

Prompt 1: Students should write a letter stating their opinion about year-round schooling. They should include reasons and support for each reason.

Prompt 2: Students should write an essay for a community newspaper in which they describe their favorite season of the year. Students should include examples to support their ideas and present information in a logical order.

Prompt 3: Students should write a real or made-up story for children about the best day they ever had. Stories should include characters, dialogue, setting, and sensory details.

NOTES